HOW THE
OPTIONS
MARKETS
WORK

Titles also in This Series

HOW THE
OPTIONS
MARKETS
WORK

Joseph A. Walker

NEW YORK INSTITUTE OF FINANCE

NEW YORK • TORONTO • SYDNEY • TOKYO • SINGAPORE

Library of Congress Cataloging-in-Publication Data

Walker, Joseph A.
    How the options markets work / Joseph A. Walker.
        p.   cm.
    Includes index.
    ISBN 0-13-400888-X
    1. Options (Finance)   I. Title.
    HG6024.A3W35   1991   90-43849
    332.63'228—dc20   CIP

Printed in the United States of America

10

This publication is designed to provide accurate and authoritative information in regard to the subject matter covered. It is sold with the understanding that the publisher is not engaged in rendering legal, accounting, or other professional service. If legal advice or other expert assistance is required, the services of a competent professional person should be sought.
—*From the Declaration of Principles jointly adopted by a Committee of the American Bar Association and a Committee of Publishers and Associations*

The following figures have been reprinted with permission.

Figures 3.1, 10.1, and 10.2 reprinted by permission of *The Wall Street Journal*, © Dow Jones & Company, Inc. 1990. All Rights Reserved Worldwide.

ISBN 0-13-400888-X

ATTENTION: CORPORATIONS AND SCHOOLS

NYIF books are available at quantity discounts with bulk purchase for educational, business, or sales promotional use. For information, please write to: Prentice Hall Career & Personal Development Special Sales, 240 Frisch Court, Paramus, New Jersey 07652. Please supply: title of book, ISBN number, quantity, how the book will be used, date needed.

NEW YORK INSTITUTE OF FINANCE
Paramus, NJ 07652

A Simon & Schuster Company

On the World Wide Web at http://www.phdirect.com

Prentice-Hall International (UK) Limited, *London*
Prentice-Hall of Australia Pty. Limited, *Sydney*
Prentice-Hall Canada Inc., *Toronto*
Prentice-Hall Hispanoamericana, S.A., *Mexico*
Prentice-Hall of India Private Limited, *New Delhi*
Prentice-Hall of Japan, Inc., *Tokyo*
Simon & Schuster Asia Pte. Ltd., *Singapore*
Editora Prentice-Hall do Brasil, Ltda., *Rio de Janeiro*

Contents

CHAPTER 9
Equity Options Margin, 133

CHAPTER 10
Other Options Products, 157

CHAPTER 11
Summary, 175

Preface

Equity securities are stocks issued by a coporation to raise capital for growth and expansion. Equities can be separated into two categories—common stock and preferred stock. Once issued, they trade in the marketplace at prices that will rise and fall depending on the opinion of the investing public regarding the corporation's future.

Options on equity securities are an entirely different product. They are not issued by corporations and provide no capital for industry. Options are simply contracts that allow the owner of the contract to purchase or sell a particular common stock at a stated price. The one who sells the contract agrees to accommodate the buyer if the latter chooses to exercise his right (option).

While options have played a role in securities markets for decades, they did not become a major factor until 1973, when they began to trade actively on stock exchanges. Prior to that time, the options market was not centralized, and only professional investors and traders dealt in these products.

Following their listing on exchanges, options trading volume has soared, and individual investors as well as professionals have contributed to that market's growth.

Yet options remain the most misunderstood product in the investment world. Many investors find them mysterious and shy away from them as some diners might shun exotic food in a foreign restaurant. Such sideliners will never experience the potential joy that can be achieved, but neither will they experience the possible pain.

Options are not for everyone, and it is not the purpose of this book to recommend their use. But failure to understand options leaves an unnecessary void in one's total knowledge of investments. Because options trading affects other securities markets, investors and students of investing should have a working knowledge of this unique financial product.

How the Options Markets Work will provide a basic understanding of:

What equity options are and what they are not

How they are created and how they trade in the market

The uses to which they can be put by both conservative and speculative investors

The potential rewards, and the large, often unlimited, risks which options represent

At first look, options seem to be very complicated devices. In fact, they are quite simple to understand once one becomes accustomed to the terminology. It's similar to learning a foreign language. Once the vocabulary is in place, the application of the words becomes easy.

CHAPTER 1

The Language of Options

Perhaps the best way to understand what an equity option is would be to understand what it is not. An option is not a security. Options on General Motors stock are not authorized or issued by General Motors Corporation. An option is simply a contract entered into by two parties. One party is the buyer of the contract, the other party is the seller.

Suppose you own a house in the country that is currently worth $100,000. You might enter into a contract with someone that would allow that person a chance to purchase your house for $100,000 during the period of one year. You sell the contract, the other party purchases it. In selling this contract, you are aware that the value of the house could change over the next twelve months. Perhaps it may rise in value to $120,000. Under the terms of your contract, you would be required to sell the house for $100,000 if the other party exercised his right to purchase. For accepting this risk, you demand payment of a fee from the other party. Perhaps the buyer pays you $5,000 as a consideration for your granting him this privilege to lock in today's price. If the value of the property were to rise to $120,000 within the year, the buyer of the contract would probably exercise his right and buy it for $100,000. You would actually receive $105,000, the contract price plus the fee, but the buyer would still get a bargain.

But suppose during the year the price of the house declined to $90,000. The buyer certainly would not pay you $100,000, and the contract would expire. This time you are the winner because you keep the $5,000 fee and still own the house.

Options are no different. In the options market, a contract is written giving the buyer of the contract the right (*option*) to purchase or sell a particular security at a fixed price for a period of time. The seller agrees to deliver if the contract owner elects to buy, or to purchase if the contract owner elects to sell. For agreeing to the terms of the contract, the seller receives a fee, which in options is called the *premium*.

Suppose the common stock of IBM is trading in the market at $115 a share. A contract (option) might be written allowing the buyer of this contract to purchase 100 shares of IBM stock at $115 at any time over the next three months. The seller will have agreed to deliver the 100 shares at this price on demand. For granting this option, the seller is paid a fee (premium) of perhaps 8. This fee translates into $800 – $8 a share for each of the 100 shares covered by the contract.

If, within the next three months, IBM stock rises to $130 a share, the option contract will be exercised by the buyer. He will have purchased 100 shares of IBM at $123 a share ($115 contract price plus $8 per share premium) which is well below the $130 market price.

If the stock had declined to $95 a share during the three-month period, the owner of the contract would do nothing. He will certainly not pay $115 a share for stock worth only $95. The contract will expire. The seller of the contract will keep the $800 premium. The buyer will be out $800.

This example illustrates an options contract which gave the owner the right to purchase stock. Options can also be devised that give the owner the right to sell stock at a fixed price.

So it comes down to this. The purchaser of an option has the privilege to buy or sell a security under specific terms. For this privilege he pays a fee. The seller of an option has taken on an obligation to accommodate the buyer. For accepting this obligation he receives the fee. While there are limitless ways of applying options to investment strategies, these are the basic, simple points:

An option is a contract between two parties

The buyer receives a privilege for which he pays a fee

The seller accepts an obligation for which he receives a fee

Although options have been a part of the securities market for many years, they did not become a major factor until 1973, the year options began to be traded on an exchange. The Chicago Board of Trade, known worldwide for the trading of commodity futures, established a subsidiary called the Chicago Board Options Exchange (CBOE).

Initially, the trading was limited to options covering only twenty-five stocks. In time, that has expanded to options on the stocks of more than five hundred companies. In addition to the CBOE, equity options are also listed on the American Stock Exchange, the Philadelphia Stock Exchange, the Pacific Stock Exchange, and the New York Stock Exchange.

The popularity of equity options led to the creation of options on other products. Options are now available on market indexes such as the Standard & Poor's 500 Stock Index, on foreign currencies such as Japanese yen, and on debt instruments of the U.S. Treasury. These other options products will be discussed later in this book, but our main concern is the study of options on equity securities.

TYPES OF OPTIONS

There are only two types of options—*puts* and *calls*. Although there are always two parties to an options contract, they are always defined from the standpoint *of the buyer* (owner) of the contract.

A *put* gives the holder the right to *sell* a specific number of shares (generally 100 shares) of an agreed security at a fixed price for a period of time.

A client purchases the following option:

1 Polaroid Jan 45 Put—Premium 3¼

This contract allows the buyer of the option to sell (put) 100 shares of Polaroid common stock at $45 a share at any time between now and next January (the exact date of expiration will be discussed later). For this privilege, the buyer pays a fee (premium) of $325 ($3¼ a share for each of the 100 shares). Naturally, some other person has sold this contract and has agreed to buy 100 shares of Polaroid at $45 a share if the owner of the contract requests it. For doing this the seller has received a fee of $325.

The buyer of a put has purchased a right to sell. Sounds a bit strange, but that is what a put is. The owner of a put has the right to sell.

A *call* gives the holder the right to *buy* a specific number of shares (generally 100 shares) of an agreed security at a fixed price for a period of time.

A client purchases the following option:

1 Teledyne Nov 370 Call—Premium 10

This contract allows the buyer of the option to buy (call) 100 shares of Teledyne common stock at $370 a share at any time between now and a given date next November. For this privilege, the buyer pays a fee (premium) of $1,000 ($10 a share for each of the 100 shares).

The buyer of a call has purchased the right to buy. Again this sounds a bit odd, but it is correct. The owner of a call has the right to buy.

Let's examine some options terminology:

1 Polaroid Jan 45 Put—Premium 3¼

1 Teledyne Nov 370 Call—Premium 10

1-1	The number of contracts (100 shares each)
Polaroid-Teledyne	The underlying securities
Jan-Nov	The expiration months (January-November)
45-370	The exercise prices (also called the "strike" prices)
Put-Call	The types of options
3¼-10	The premiums—the number of dollars per share paid by the buyer to the seller

Long Seller versus Writer

The *buyer* of an option has purchased a contract. This is quite easy to understand. But the *seller* of the contract can be acting in either of *two* capacities.

In dealing with other securities, the seller can be selling long or short. Selling long means that the party owns the stock or bond and is eliminating his holding. If you owned 100 shares of Dow Chemical stock and decided to sell it, you would be selling long. However, you might sell the same Dow stock even if you did not own the shares. This is called *short selling*. In short selling, you would have to borrow the shares from some other party in order to deliver them to the buyer. Your hope is that the price of Dow shares will decline, and you will be able to purchase them at a price lower than that at which you sold them short. If you are successful, a profit will result. Short selling reverses the usual order of dealing in securities. Normally, one buys a stock, and, if it goes up in price, he sells it. The short seller sells first, and if the price declines, he gains. No matter which order you use, the result will be a profit if you were right, a loss if you were wrong.

The selling of equity options is no different. They can be sold *long* or *short*. For example, a client sells 1 Xerox Oct 45 Call—Premium 7. He had purchased this option three weeks earlier at a premium of 3. His original cost of $300 is now worth $700 (premium). He sells the call and profits by $400 less expenses. This occurs because he owned the call he was selling long. When you buy an option, you are long the option. When you sell it, you are selling long.

However, suppose a client sold 1 Xerox Oct 45 Call—Premium 7 when he did not own this option. He is selling short. In fact, he is creating this option through his short sale.

For some reason the options industry does not use the term *short seller*. Instead it uses the term *writer*. Whenever you see the word writer in connection with options, just substitute short seller.

USES OF EQUITY OPTIONS

Puts and calls can be used for a variety of purposes, but essentially there are two broad applications. They can be used conservatively to protect some other position in a security, or they can be used as a method of speculation. Let's first look at long positions (buying) of options as a means of protecting a position. We will first examine their application as a conservative investment technique.

Long Put—A Conservative Approach

Two years ago a client purchased 100 shares of Teledyne stock at $210 a share. Her investment has been very rewarding as the price of Teledyne is now $370 a share. She expects that Teledyne will continue to rise in price and her profit will increase. But she is a bit concerned. Remembering the severe market decline of October 1987, she wishes to protect her position. What might she do?

Buy 1 TDY Jan 370 Put — Premium 8

This client has now protected her position until the following January. Should a major decline in the price of Teledyne occur, she will exercise her put.

EXAMPLE: Teledyne drops in price to $280 a share. Our client will exercise her put and sell the stock at the strike price of $370. Naturally, she must allow for the $800 premium cost of the put so that her true proceeds will be only $362 a share, but that sure beats the current price of $280. Even if the price of

Teledyne does not fall but rises in value, our client should be wearing a smile.

EXAMPLE: Teledyne rises in price to $400 a share. Our client will not exercise her put and sell at the $370 strike price. No, the option will be allowed to expire, and she will forfeit $800 paid in premium. But her long position in the stock is now worth $400 a share, a full $30 more per share than when she purchased the put. She has made an additional $3,000 ($30 per share on 100 shares) at the sacrifice of the $800 put premium. A very pleasing situation. If the stock price had gone down, she would have been protected by owning the put. If the stock rose in value, she would have profited on the stock and lost the premium.

The term premium is a very accurate description of the situation. Our client bought "insurance" and paid a premium. If things went poorly, the insurance (put), was there to protect her. If things went well, the insurance became unnecessary. We all pay premiums on life insurance to protect our loved ones, but we are not anxious for them to collect.

Long Call—A Conservative Approach

A client believed that IBM stock was going to decline in value. To profit from this opinion, he sold *short* 100 shares of IBM at $115 a share. He does not own the stock but hopes it will drop to $90 a share. At that point he will purchase stock at that price and show a profit of $25 a share against his short sale price of $115.

But suppose he is wrong. IBM stock does not go down but goes up to $200 a share. The short seller may be forced to purchase the shares at that price to cover the short sale at $115. A loss of $85 a share would result. There is no limit to the amount of potential loss that can result from a short sale. The shares could rise to $200, $300, or even $500 a share. How high is up? The short seller would eventually be forced to purchase the shares. What might he do?

Buy 1 IBM Feb 115 Call — Premium 5

Our client is now protected until next February.

EXAMPLE: If IBM rises to $200 a share, the client will exercise his call and buy the stock at $115. He has covered the short sale made at that same price, so his loss is only the $500 premium paid to purchase the call.

EXAMPLE: If the stock had dropped to $90 a share, our client could have bought 100 shares at that price for a profit of $25 a share against the short sale made at $115. From this we must subtract the $500 premium paid, but it still represents a successful transaction. The "insurance" (option) was not used, but it provided the protection and prevented sleepless nights.

In summary, a client desiring to protect a current position by using long puts or long calls would do the following:

Client is Long (owner) stock = Buy Puts

Client is Short Stock = Buy Calls

Now that we have looked at the conservative use of buying puts and calls to protect a position, let's study their use as a means of speculation.

Long Put—A Speculative Approach

A student of the market came to the conclusion that the stock of Texas Instruments, selling at $90 a share, was about to suffer a decline in price. To take advantage of this opinion, he could choose between two courses of action:

1. Sell Texas Instruments stock *short*

2. Buy Texas Instruments puts

Let's look at the potential risks and rewards of these different approaches. Sell 100 shares Texas Instruments @90 short.

1. It is conceivable, though unlikely, that this transaction could result in a profit of $9,000. The short sale at $90 a share would produce proceeds of $9,000 (100 shares sold at $90 a share). If Texas Instruments went out of business and its stock became worthless, the short seller could acquire the stock free and return the shares to the party from whom he originally borrowed them when making the short sale. He sold short for proceeds of $9,000 and purchased for $0, hence a $9,000 profit. A decline in price below $90 would represent some profit, but $9,000 is the maximum possibility.

However, we must also consider the negatives involved in the short sale. Under Federal Reserve margin regulations, a client selling short must deposit with his broker an amount equal to a minimum of 50% of the proceeds of the sale. In our example, the short sale of Texas Instruments would require a deposit of at least $4,500. This represents a substantial commitment of the client's funds.

But the major risk of a short sale is the potential for an unlimited loss. When a person sells stock short, he borrows the shares from someone to make delivery. This process is arranged by his broker. At some point he must repurchase those shares and return them to the lender. If he buys at $100 a share ($10,000 for 100 shares), he loses $1,000, as he sold at $90 a share ($9,000). Suppose he must buy at $110, $120, or $200. For every point Texas Instruments rises above $90, our client loses $100. As there is no limit to how far the stock can rise, there is no limit to his potential loss.

It is important to remember that a short seller must repurchase the shares at some point in time. If he buys below the price of the short sale, he profits. If he must pay above the short sale price, he loses.

The short seller has sold something that he does not own. At some point he must purchase the shares. There is a quote that was applied to many famous short sellers of the 1920s, which puts the facts into perspective:

> "He that sells what isn't his'n
> Buys it back or goes to prison."

2. Let's look at our client's other choice:

Buy 1 Texas Instruments July 90 Put—Premium 5

This option would give our client the right to sell (put) 100 shares of Texas Instruments at $90 a share until next July. His total outlay of cash would be the $500 premium, much less than the $4,500 deposit for the short sale. If he is correct and Texas Instruments stock declines to $70 a share, he can purchase 100 shares at that price and exercise his put at $90. He bought at $70, sold at $90 for a gross profit of $2,000 (20 points on 100 shares). We subtract the $500 premium, leaving a net profit of $1,500.

If the client proves to be wrong, and Texas Instruments rises in price, his maximum loss is the $500 premium paid for the option. By purchasing the put rather than selling the stock short, the client reduced his cash outlay to $500 and limited his potential loss to that same amount. When a client buys an option, the *maximum* loss is the premium paid for the contract.

There is one major drawback to buying options that must be considered. *Options expire.* In our second example, for our client to profit, the price of Texas Instruments must decline. But it must do so before the end of next July when the put expires. If the stock declines to $50 a share next August, it is too late to help our client. His put expired in July. All he has is a sad story to relate at his

Friday night bridge game. Had he sold the stock short, he might still be able to repurchase the shares at $50 and record a nice 40 point ($4,000) profit.

In buying options as a speculator you must not only be right, but you must be right *within a specific period of time.*

Long Call—A Conservative Approach

Let us assume that a follower of the stock market comes to the conclusion that the common stock of Coca Cola, now trading at $60 a share, is about to rise sharply in price. To profit from this expectation she might take either of the following positions:

1. Buy Coca Cola stock

2. Buy Coca Cola calls

Let's analyze these two choices as to the potential risks and rewards.

B 100 shares Coca Cola @ 60

This position offers an unlimited potential profit. As our client bought the stock at $60 a share, any increase in value above that price represents a profit to her. How high is up? The stock could rise to $80, $100, or $300 a share. There is no limit.

There are, of course, negatives. She must deposit a minimum of $3,000 (50% of the $6,000 cost) under margin regulations. She would borrow the balance ($3,000) from her broker and pay interest on the loan. She also faces the possibility of losing as much as $6,000. If Coca Cola stock becomes worthless, she loses the total cost of the purchase. We recognize that this is most improbable, but it is possible. Let's now look at the alternative.

Buy 1 Coca Cola April 60 Call—Premium 4½

Our client now has the right (option) to purchase (call) 100 shares of Coca Cola stock at $60 a share. This privilege cost her $450 (4½ premium for 100 shares). If she is wrong and Coca Cola stock goes down, she can lose no more than the $450 premium. Her potential profit is unlimited. She has the option to purchase Coke stock at $60 a share. Suppose it rises to $90 or $150? She exercises her call and buys at $60 and sells at the higher price. She profits by the amount of the price increase less the $450 premium paid.

As opposed to buying the stock, buying the call required a much smaller cash outlay while providing almost as much potential for profit. The buyer cannot lose more than $450. Buying the stock allowed for a potential loss of up to $6,000.

But again we must remember that options expire. The client must be correct in her opinion that Coke stock will rise in price, and she must be right by next April. If the price goes up to $100 a share next May, it will be too late to do her any good. Had she bought the 100 shares, she might still own them and be able to sell and take a profit.

It's very difficult to be correct in the analysis of stock prices. Options present a second obstacle. You must be right within a limited time period.

We have looked at the buying of options as a means of protecting positions and as a speculation. Now let us study the writing (shorting) of puts and calls. The writing of options is usually done in conjunction with other security or options positions. We will discuss these later when we study advanced options positions. But as a basic strategy, writing puts and calls is generally used as a form of speculation.

Short Put

Suppose an investor believes that Coca Cola stock, currently trading at $60, is about to rise in price. As we described earlier, she might profit if she purchased the stock or if she bought a call on the stock. Another method to profit from a rise in price would be to write a put on Coca Cola stock.

EXAMPLE: Write 1 Coca Cola April 60 Put—Premium 4½.

Upon writing the put, the investor receives a premium of $450. If, as she expects, the stock rises, let's say to $70, the owner of the put would not exercise against her. The owner would not sell (put) at the strike price of $60 when the market price is $70. The put option will expire, and our writer will keep the $450. If she turns out to be wrong, she has a risk of a large loss. Suppose, unlikely as it is, that Coca Cola stock becomes worthless. She will be put and required to buy 100 shares at $60 a share ($6,000). As it is now worthless, she has a net loss of $5,550. This represents the $6,000 loss on the stock minus the $450 premium received for writing the put.

Writing this put creates a position with a maximum profit of $450 and a potential loss of $5,550. A very risky situation not to be considered by the average individual investor.

Note: In Chapter 2 we will study the difference between *covered* writing and *uncovered* writing of options. Covered writing reduces the risks, but the maximum risk presumes the writer is uncovered.

Short Call

Texas Instruments stock is trading at $90 a share. An investor concludes that this price will decline. As stated earlier, he could sell the stock short or purchase a put on the stock. A third choice would be to write (short) a call on Texas Instruments stock.

EXAMPLE: Write 1 Texas Instruments July 90 Call—Premium 5

The sale of this call brings $500 in premium to the writer. If the stock declines to $80, the buyer of the call will not exercise and pay $90. Our writer keeps the $500 premium. The risk of loss, however, is unlimited. For example, suppose Texas Instruments reports a huge increase in earnings, and the stock rises to $120, $220, or even higher. Our client has written a call with a strike price of $90 a share. The owner will exercise, and the writer must sell him, 100 shares at $90 a share. If the writer does not have access to the stock, he must buy it in the open market at whatever the current price happens to be. Therefore, his risk of loss is potentially unlimited. Writing this call created these current possibilities:

Maximum profit: $500 premium

Maximum loss: unlimited

When faced with this maximum loss potential, the writing of calls should be marked "For Professional Use Only."

We know what an investor would do in the stock market if she thought a particular stock was about to rise in value. She would buy the stock. In the options market, there are two methods of taking advantage of a rising price:

Long (Buy)—Calls

Short (Write)—Puts

In a declining market an investor would consider shorting a stock. Again the options market provides two opportunities to profit from a price decline:

Long (Buy)—Puts

Short (Write)—Calls

As we have shown, these positions differ greatly as to the possible risks and rewards. Table 1.1 illustrates these differences.

It is clear that the long position offers less risk and greater rewards than the short position. But the history of options tells us that most options are not exercised. Therefore, the writer (short seller) retains the premium.

EXAMPLE: 1 GM Nov 80 Call

Aggregate exercise price is $8,000. If the call is exercised, the holder buys the stock and pays the writer $80 a share for 100 shares.

EXAMPLE: 1 EK June 45 Put

If exercised, the holder delivers 100 shares of Eastman Kodak to the writer who pays $45 a share or $4,500 in aggregate exercise price.

In many cases, the client who purchases options does not do so with the intention of exercising the option. His goal is simply to make a profit by selling the option if the value of the premium increases. In fact, the client may not have the financial resources to exercise even if he should wish to do so.

Table 1.1. Long vs. Short Risks/Rewards

Position	Maximum Profit	Maximum Loss
Long put	Exercise value* minus premium	Premium
Long call	Unlimited	Premium
Short put	Premium	Exercise value* minus premium
Short call	Premium	Unlimited

*The exercise value of an option, usually called the aggregate exercise price, represents the amount of money that would change hands if an option were to be exercised.

EXAMPLE: Customer A believes that the price of CBS stock is going to rise and he wishes to profit from this occurrence. The price of the stock is $180 a share and he cannot afford to purchase many shares of the stock. To buy 1,000 shares requires an outlay of about $180,000. Even if purchased on 50% margin, he would need $90,000 and would incur a debt of an additional $90,000. Neither of these choices is within his means.

He looks at CBS options and discovers that the CBS Jun 180 calls can be purchased at 2. He can buy 10 of these calls at a cost of $2,000 ($200 for each option) and share in the profit of a rise in the stock price. Best of all, he can afford to invest $2,000. He enters his order and buys: 10 CBS Jun 180 Calls @ 2.

The client's forecast is correct and shortly before expiration, CBS stock rises to $185. If the calls are exercised, he will have to come up with the aggregate exercise value of $180,000 or the appropriate margin. As he is unable to do this, he sells the calls.

Since the stock is at 185, the options have an intrinsic value of $5. They should be trading in the market at approximately that price because expiration is so near. He sells the 10 calls—assume at $5—and receives $500 for each or a total of $5,000.

The result is quite gratifying as his gross profit is $3,000. His cost of purchase was only $2,000, so this represents a profit of 150%. He benefited handsomely without exercising the calls.

The same rationale applies to puts. If a client thought that IBM stock would decline from its current market value of $110 a share, he might purchase puts. Should the shares fall in value, the put premium will increase.

He enters the following order:

Buy 10 IBM Aug 110 Puts @ 2½

If the order is executed, he will own puts on 1,000 shares of IBM at $110 a share. The cost to him will be the premium of $2,500 ($250 for each option). As the August date of expiration nears, IBM stock declines to $100 a share. If he exercises the puts, he will deliver 1,000 shares and be paid a total of $110,000. But our client does not own the stock. To accomplish delivery he will have to go into the market and buy the shares. But the cost of $100,000 (1,000 shares at $100) is much more than he can afford. So he sells the put options. If it is close to the expiration date, the puts should be worth a premium of about 10. These options grant the privilege to sell at $110 a share. The market price is $100 a share. They are 10 points "in the money." If he sells at this price, the proceeds of the sale are $10,000. When measured against his cost of $2,500, his reward has been most generous.

The owner of an option has three choices:

1. The option can be exercised

2. The option can be sold

3. The option can be allowed to expire

Choices 1 and 2 can result in either a profit or loss. Choice 3 always results in a loss.

But at least the buyer has choices. The writer of an equity options contract has only an obligation. If a call is exercised against him he *must* deliver the stock. If a put is exercised against him he *must* purchase the stock. The premium is his fee for accepting this obligation.

CHAPTER 2

Covered versus Uncovered Writing

If you purchase an equity option, you are said to be *long* in the contract. If, at a later point, you elect to sell the option you are selling long.

But as discussed in the last chapter, a seller may be selling an option that he does not own. This is called *selling short*. In the language of options, however, the short seller is called the *writer* of the option.

A distinction in writing an option is the difference between a *covered* writer as opposed to an *uncovered* writer. This difference is quite important as the uncovered writer faces a large, potentially unlimited risk while the covered writer has reduced that risk and may, in fact, incur no risk at all.

We can compare covered and uncovered writing of options contracts to the short selling of other securities.

Suppose you sold 100 shares of IBM common stock at 110. At the time of this sale, you did not own any IBM stock. This would be a short sale, the sale of something that you did not own. But suppose you owned some IBM convertible bonds, which could, at your election, be exchanged for 100 shares of stock. Should IBM stock rise in price to 130 a share, your short sale would represent a loss of 20 points. If you repurchased the shares at 130 against the short sale at 110, you would be a loser by that difference in price. In fact, the stock could rise still higher to 150, 200, or 300. With each increase of 1 point, the loss on your short sale grows by $100. But in this situation you have an offsetting position. If the short position becomes a problem, you can convert your IBM bonds into 100 shares of stock. These shares can then be delivered to close out the short sale and end your position. The profit or loss would depend on the price you had paid for the convertible bonds. You received $11,000 (110 a share) for the short sale of the stock. If you paid less for the bonds you have a profit. If you paid more, you have a loss

In this example we have used convertible bonds. Most companies do not issue this type of security, however, protection on the short sale of a stock would be provided if you owned any exchangeable security. In addition to convertible bonds, you would be protected if you owned a sufficient amount of convertible preferred stock, warrants, or options on the stock sold short.

If a client wrote an option under similar circumstances, we would define him as a *covered* writer. He does not own the option, but if it is exercised against him, he has some other position which would reduce or perhaps eliminate his risk.

If there were no offsetting position, the writer would be

uncovered (sometimes called *naked*). If the option were exercised, he would have to purchase the security to make delivery (call) or put up the money to accept delivery (put).

In summary, *the writer of a covered put or call has limited risk.*

The writer of an uncovered put or call has a large potential loss. Writing an uncovered put could result in a loss equal to the aggregate exercise price less the premium received.

The writer of a naked call assumes an unlimited loss possibility.

EXAMPLE: Write (Uncovered) 1 Westinghouse Jan 70 Put—Premium 3¼. Potential loss = $6,675.

Westinghouse stock becomes worthless. The writer is put at 70 and must purchase 100 shares for $7,000. This loss is offset only by the $325 premium received to write the put. Net loss = $6,675.

EXAMPLE: Write (Uncovered) 1 American Airlines Feb 105 Call—Premium 10 Potential Loss = Unlimited.

There is no limit to how high American Airlines stock can rise. If the call is exercised, the writer would have to purchase the stock and deliver at $105 a share. The only offset to his loss would be the $1,000 premium received when he wrote the call.

We must look at the offsetting positions that create a covered writer.

COVERED CALLS

The writer of a call is considered to be covered if she has any of the following offsetting positions:

Long the stock

Bank escrow receipt

Convertible security

Warrants

Long a call on the same stock

EXAMPLE: Write 1 Holiday Corp. Nov 80 Call—Premium 5.

The writer would be covered if:

1. She owned 100 shares of Holiday Corp. stock. If called, her broker could deliver the shares from her account.

2. She deposited an escrow receipt with her broker from a bank which stated that they held 100 shares of Holiday Corp. in her account and would deliver the shares upon request.

3. She owned Holiday Corp. convertible bonds or convertible preferred stock. If called, her broker could exchange the convertible security for the common stock and deliver against the exercise.

4. She owned sufficient warrants to purchase 100 shares of this stock. If exercised, the broker could exercise the warrants and accomplish delivery.

5. She owns a call on Holiday Corp. stock. If the call that she wrote is exercised against her, she would exercise her own call and deliver the stock that she receives.

In this last situation it is important to note that to be covered, the call that she *owns* cannot expire earlier than the one that she *wrote* and must have an exercise price equal to or lower than the option written.

EXAMPLE:

Write 1 Holiday Corp. Nov 80 Call
Long 1 Holiday Corp. Dec 80 Call

This is a covered position. If the November 80 call is exercised against the client, she will exercise the December 80 call. She buys 100 shares at 80 and delivers 100 shares at 80.

EXAMPLE:

Write 1 Holiday Corp. Nov 80 Call
Long 1 Holiday Corp. Oct 80 Call

This is an uncovered position as the call she is long expires earlier (October) than the call that she wrote (November). What happens during that additional month? The risk is unlimited, as she no longer has an offsetting position.

EXAMPLE:

Write 1 Holiday Corp. Nov 80 Call
Long 1 Holiday Corp. Nov 90 Call

This, too, is an uncovered position as the strike price on the call she owns (90) is higher than the strike price on the call that she wrote (80). If exercised, she must deliver stock at $80 a share. If she exercises her own call, she must pay $90 a share. As this creates a risk, the position is considered to be uncovered.

An easy way to distinguish between covered and uncovered writing is:

Covered writing does not put the broker handling the client's account at risk.

Uncovered writing does put the broker handling the account at risk.

As we will see later in our study, options positions are recorded in the name of the broker handling the account. If an option is exercised, it is the broker who must receive or deliver the shares. The broker then looks to the client for completion of the transaction. If there is any risk to the broker, the option is uncovered, and the client must provide protection. That protection is determined under the margin requirements covering options transactions.

COVERED PUTS

There is only one position that allows a client to write a covered put. She must be long a put on the *same* stock that does not expire earlier than the one written and that has a strike price equal to or higher than the short put.

EXAMPLE:
> Write 1 Digital Equip Dec 90 Put
> Long 1 Digital Equip Dec 95 Put

This position is covered as the expiration months are the same (December) and the strike price on the long put (95) is higher than the short put (90).

If the worst were to happen, and Digital stock declined to zero, our client would be put and required to buy stock at 90. But she would then exercise her long put and sell at 95. A 5-point profit would result. There is no risk to the broker. This put is covered.

EXAMPLE:
> Write 1 Digital Equip Dec 90 Put
> Long 1 Digital Equip Nov 90 Put

The client has written an uncovered put. Her long position is one month shorter than the put she wrote. This creates risk for the broker. The put is uncovered.

EXAMPLE:

    Write 1 Digital Equip Dec 90 Put
    Long 1 Digital Equip Dec 85 Put

This is an uncovered put as there is a risk of 5 points. If both puts are exercised, she must buy at 90 and has the right to sell at 85. Though the risk is small, only 5 points, a risk does exist; therefore the position is uncovered.

We will detail the margin rules covering equity options in Chapter 9, but for the moment let us state that if a client writes a covered option, there is no risk to the broker. Therefore no margin will be required. As an uncovered option does create risk, the client will be required to deposit margin.

USING COVERED CALLS

Covered calls are often used by clients to protect positions and to increase income. Individual investors might find this practice to be useful in managing their portfolios. This device does not increase risk, in fact, it reduces it, but it does have a negative factor in that it can reduce the potential for profit.

A client purchases 100 shares of Exxon common stock at $42 a share.

He then writes the following option:

Write 1 Exxon Jan 45 Call — Premium 2½

As he owns the stock, this is a covered call and by writing it he has reduced his potential loss on the stock. He could sell the stock 2½ points below his cost and still break-even as this loss would be offset by the premium received for writing the call:

Cost of stock	42
Less option premium	2½
Break-even point	39½

The negative factor is that he has limited his potential profit on the stock.

If Exxon stock rises to $50 a share, the call that he wrote will be exercised against him, and he will have to sell at $45. To this we add the 2½ point premium that he received, making his actual sale price 47½.

Exercise price	45
Plus premium received	2½
Sale price	47½

But the stock is at $50 a share. Had he not written the call, he could sell at that price and increase his profit. But in all, the position has been profitable. He purchased the stock at 42 and sold at 47½ for an overall profit of 5½ points. Though the profit would have been greater had he not written the call, a nice profit does result.

Writing covered calls can also be used to produce additional income from a position. Suppose Exxon stock does not rise above 45 before expiration in January. The call will not be exercised, and our writer will keep the $250 premium. He might then write an April 45 call and collect another premium of perhaps $250. If this call also expires unexercised, he adds another $250 to his account.

In the months wherein he held the Exxon stock, he was also receiving dividends. If Exxon paid $2.40 a share in dividends each year, it would be paid in quarterly installments of 60 cents a share. We may presume that in six months he will have received two dividends totaling $1.20 a share or $120. Add to this the two premiums received, and he has collected a total of $620.

January call premium	$250
April call premium	250
Dividends ($1.20 a share)	120
Total	$620

Obviously, the stock could have been called away from him at any time, but if the options are not exercised he continues to collect the dividends.

Covered call writing has many applications. It can be used to provide downside protection for stocks that you own, and can increase your income. It will also limit your potential profit. As in any investment decision, you must weigh the positives and the negatives.

WRITING UNCOVERED PUTS

While writing uncovered options is always a dangerous strategy, there are times when this device can be used to accomplish an objective that is in itself conservative. One example is the use of naked put writing as a means of purchasing a security at a favorable price.

Assume that Dow Chemical stock is trading at $102 a share. A client wishes to purchase 1,000 shares, but thinks that the price will soon decline to $100 a share or slightly lower.

The usual procedure would be to place a limit order to buy the stock.

The following order might be placed with his broker:

Buy 1,000 Dow Chemical @ 100

This order would be entered on the floor of the New York Stock Exchange, and, as time came to pass, one of two things would happen.

1. Dow stock would decline to $100 a share or less, and he would purchase the 1,000 shares.

2. Dow stock would not decline to $100 a share and he would be left with nothing but an unexecuted order.

27

In each case there are negative possibilities. If he does purchase the stock at 100, that becomes his cost for the shares. Any decline below that price represents an instant loss. If the stock does not decline and his order is not executed, he has nothing to show for his efforts.

Using options, we might try a different approach and enter this order instead:

Write (uncovered) 10 Dow Dec 100 Puts — Premium 3

Again the same two possibilities exist:

1. Dow declines below $100, and the puts are exercised against our client causing him to purchase 1,000 shares of Dow at 100 a share.

2. Dow does not decline, and the options are not exercised.

In the second case, there are compensations to the put option writer that were not available by simply placing an order to buy the stock. If the options are exercised, this client will purchase the stock at $100, but from this the premium received is subtracted, giving him an actual cost of 97. He does not suffer any loss unless the stock declines below this price.

If the options are not exercised, he does not purchase the shares, but he keeps the $3,000 premium received for writing the puts.

By writing naked puts in lieu of placing a buy order, the client reduces his cost if he is exercised, and he receives a premium for his trouble if the stock is not purchased.

Naturally, he still has risk. If he buys the stock and it drops below 97, he will suffer a loss. However, even this possibility is more acceptable than suffering a loss if the stock fell below 100.

The variety of uses of equity options leads to many possible strategies. We will discuss a number of them in Chapters 6 and 7. But it is important to understand that while options often create great risk, they can just as often be used to reduce or eliminate risk created by alternative positions.

Any investment includes risk. Each investor must decide how much risk he can afford to take both financially and psychologically.

CHAPTER 3

Trading of Equity Options

Now that the basic types and uses of equity options have been introduced, the method employed in trading this product will be explored.

Options have existed in the market for decades, but prior to 1973 the trading was done on a very informal and decentralized basis. If a client of Merrill Lynch wished to purchase a call on IBM stock, Merrill would contact a put and call dealer. There were many such firms, most of which were small entities. At Merrill's request they would attempt to find someone willing to write the IBM call. After a search they might find a writer, but all terms of the contract had to be agreed upon.

For instance, the Merrill client might wish to purchase a call expiring in March. The writer might prefer a February expiration.

The buyer might want a strike price of 110 while the seller would only agree to a 115 strike.

Merrill's buyer might be willing to pay a premium of 5 ($500). The writer might demand 5½ ($550). All of these differences have to be eliminated before a contract can be agreed upon.

The year 1973 brought about a major change in the options market. It was in that year that equity options began to trade on stock exchanges. This centralized the market and eliminated many of the prior difficulties.

The first trading in equity options on exchanges began in Chicago, and to this day that city does the largest volume of trading. The Chicago Board of Trade, well-known for dealing in commodities, established a subsidiary, the Chicago Board Options Exchange (CBOE). The CBOE initiated trading in equity options on only 25 stocks. In fact in the beginning only calls were traded. Puts did not arrive on the CBOE until some time later.

In time, equity options also became listed on four other exchanges:

The American Stock Exchange (ASE)

The Philadelphia Stock Exchange (PE)

The Pacific Stock Exchange (PSE)

The New York Stock Exchange (NYSE)

At this writing, the five options exchanges provide facilities for trading both puts and calls covering approximately 500 underlying securities.

The success of the listed market for equity options has led

to the development of options on other underlying products. Options now trade on stock indexes, foreign currencies, and U.S. Treasury securities.

With the listing of equity options, two of the three important characteristics of each option were determined by the exchange on which the option is listed. Both the *strike price* and the *expiration month* are determined by the exchange. Only the *premium* remains to be negotiated by the buyer and seller of the contract.

EXPIRATION MONTHS

Options are traded with three different expiration months. There is always a contract expiring in the current month and one in the following month. So if the current month were June, there would always be a June and a July expiration. The third month would depend on the cycle in which the option is listed.

There are three options cycles, the January cycle, the February cycle, and the March cycle. Each cycle contains four months—the cycle month plus three others.

Cycle	Jan	Feb	Mar
	Apr	May	Jun
	July	Aug	Sept
	Oct	Nov	Dec

The third expiration month that would be trading at any point in time is the next available month in each cycle.

For example, presuming the current month is June, the third month of trading for June in each cycle would consist of October (from the January cycle); August (from the February cycle); and September (from the March cycle). Thus trading in each cycle would consist of the following months:

Cycle	Jan	Feb	Mar
	Jun	Jun	Jun
	July	July	July
	Oct	Aug	Sept

This standardization permits trading to be concentrated in the available months. If at this time a client wished to buy a GM call expiring in May, she would find that no such contract was available on the exchanges.

STRIKE PRICES

The strike prices are established by the exchanges and are generally set five points apart. On high-priced stocks the interval between strikes can be 10 points and on lower priced stocks it may be only 2½ points.

The number of available strike prices on each security depends on the volatility of that particular stock. It is important to have available a strike price that is close to the current market price. This encourages trading, as it provides for a more reasonable premium. As the price rises or falls, the exchange will add new strike prices.

If a new option is listed on a stock trading at $37 a share, the exchange will introduce two strike prices. One will be below the current price and one will be above it. For example:

	Strike
XYZ	35
37	40

If XYZ rises to $43 a share a 45 strike will be added:

	Strike
XYZ	35
43	40
43	45

The more volatile the price movement, the more strike prices that will be made available. Stocks that trade in a very narrow range may need only two strike prices. Those with wide price variations might have a dozen or more.

With the strike prices and expiration months established by the exchange, only the premium becomes a subject of negotiation. There are a number of factors that determine the premium, and many sophisticated methods have been devised to uncover values. But the three basic factors that determine an option premium are:

1. Intrinsic value

2. Time value

3. Volatility

Intrinsic value is an option's arithmetically determinable value based on the strike price of the option and the market value of the underlying stock.

EXAMPLE: Syntex stock is selling at $47¼ a share. A Syntex call with a strike price of 45 would have an intrinsic value of 2¼ points. The call gives the holder the right to purchase the stock at $45 a share. As the market value is 47¼, the call has a value of 2¼ points based solely on these price differences.

EXAMPLE: Merck stock is trading at $78 a share. A put on Merck stock with a strike price of 80 has an intrinsic value of 2 points. The stock could be purchased at 78 and sold (put) at 80. (*Note:* An option's intrinsic value is usually referred to as the "In the Money" amount.)

Time value reflects the fact that the longer the option has to run until expiration, the greater the premium should be. This is perfectly logical. The right to buy or sell a stock for two months should be worth more than the same privilege for only one month. You would have thirty or so additional days to be proven correct.

EXAMPLE: With Syntex trading at 47¼, a call with a strike price of 45 has an intrinsic value of 2¼ points. In addition to reflecting this value, the premium will also reflect the time value of the option.

A Syntex 45 call expiring in November had a premium of 3⅜ (2¼ points intrinsic value, 1⅛ points time value). The same Syntex 45 call expiring in December had a premium of 3⅞ (2¼ points intrinsic value, 1⅝ points time value).

The market is telling us that in this case the extra month of time is worth ½ point of premium value.

EXAMPLE: If Alcoa stock is trading at 78¾, an Alcoa 80 put has an intrinsic value of 1¼ points. But an Alcoa put expiring in November might have a premium of 2 (1¼ points intrinsic value, ¾ point time value). The same put expiring in January might command a premium of 3⅝ (or 1¼ points intrinsic value, 2⅜ points time value). The January option has two months longer to run than the November put. This additional time has a value. The market says that additional value is 1⅝ points.

Intrinsic value can be measured exactly. Time value is determined by the opinions of the buyers and sellers. But we must always keep in mind that options expire. Intrinsic value can remain until the last moment of an option's life. But with every tick of the clock the time value diminishes and eventually disappears.

Volatility is a factor in determining time value. Some stocks, such as public utilities, have very narrow price movements. In a recent fifty-two week period the shares of Philadelphia Electric & Gas Co. had a range of 24½–17⅛. The high for the period was about 25% up from the low price. During the same period, the stock of UAL Corp. had a high price of $294 a share which was up more than 200% from its low price of 95⅜. Given this sharp difference in volatility, one would be much more likely to recapture an option's time value in UAL than in Philadelphia Electric. The premium would reflect this.

On a given day Philadelphia Electric stock was selling at 22⅜. A Philadelphia Electric Jan 20 call has a premium of 2⅝. That premium was made up of 2⅜ points intrinsic value and ¼ point time value.

On the same day UAL Corp. stock was at 284¼. The UAL Nov 280 call had a premium of 14¼. The components were 4¼ points intrinsic value, 10 points time value. Though it expired two months sooner, the time value of the UAL call was far greater than the Philadelphia call. The reason? Volatility. While no one can predict the future, it is far more likely that UAL will move much higher in price than the shares of Philadelphia Electric will.

OPTIONS TRADING

The trading of options on exchanges is similar to the trading of stocks. Each option is assigned to a particular location on the trading floor, and negotiations between buyer and seller take place at that spot.

There are some differences in the trading procedures on the exchanges. For example, the American Stock Exchange uses the *specialist system*, which is the same as that employed in trading stocks. The *specialist* acts as both agent, buying and selling for clients, and as a principal, buying and selling for his own account. On the CBOE these functions are handled separately. The *market maker* performs solely a principal's function, trading for his own account. The *order book official* acts only as agent, handling orders for clients.

These trading distinctions are technical in nature and play no part in our understanding of the product.

Many investors have some difficulty in understanding the options tables which are published each day in the financial presses. They are quite different from the stock tables which are more familiar to most readers.

In Table 3.1 a portion of an options table for a trading day can be seen. This is only a small part of the total information but is sufficient for us to obtain an understanding of these listings. It will also allow us to introduce some frequently used options terminology.

The options page begins with a report of the previous day's trading on the CBOE.

In order to identify the items of information, let's look more closely at the listing for Honeywell options (left-hand column, Figure 3.1).

In the first column, we find the name of the underlying security, below which is the closing price of that stock on the previous day. Honeywell closed at 98.

The second column lists the available strike prices. There are five strikes for Honeywell options starting at $85 a share and moving in 5-point intervals to $105 a share.

The next three columns give us the closing premium value

Table 3.1. Reading an Options Report

Options & NY Close	Strike Price	Calls—Last			Puts—Last		
		Jun	Jul	Aug	Jun	Jul	Aug
Honwell	85	14⅜	S	r	r	S	⅜
98	90	8	r	r	r	r	r
98	95	2⅞	5⅝	7⅛	r	1¼	r
98	100	¹⁄₁₆	2⅜	4⅛	1¾	r	4
98	105	r	1	2⅛	r	r	r

Friday, June 15, 1990

Options closing prices. Sales unit usually is 100 shares. Stock close is New York or American exchange final price.

CHICAGO BOARD

Option & NY Close	Strike Price	Calls–Last Jun	Calls–Last Jul	Calls–Last Aug	Puts–Last Jun	Puts–Last Jul	Puts–Last Aug
Amdahl	15	1/8	7/8	1 3/8	r	r	r
15 1/8	17 1/2	r	5/16	1/2	r	r	r
A E P	25	5	r	4 7/8	r	r	r
29 7/8	30	r	r	1/2	r	r	r
29 7/8	35	r	r	r	5	r	r
AlnGrp	90	10	10 1/2	r	r	r	r
100 3/8	95	5 1/8	r	r	r	r	r
100 3/8	100	1/2	2 3/4	4	1/8	r	3 1/8
100 3/8	105	r	1 1/8	r	r	r	r
Amoco	50	2	r	3 1/8	r	3/8	r
52 1/8	55	r	1/4	3/4	r	r	r
52 1/8	60	r	s	1/8	r	s	r
A M P	45	6	s	r	r	s	r
51 3/8	50	1 3/8	r	r	1/16	1	r
51 3/8	55	r	1/4	5/8	4	r	r
51 3/8	60	r	1/16	r	r	r	r
Anadrk	35	r	r	1 3/8	r	r	r
33 3/4	40	r	r	1/16	r	r	r
Baxter	20	5	r	5 3/8	r	r	r
25 1/8	22 1/2	2 5/8	r	3	r	r	r
25 1/8	25	1/16	5/8	1 1/8	r	3/4	7/8
Blk Dk	12 1/2	3 1/2	r	r	r	r	r
16	15	1 1/8	1 7/16	1 3/4	r	1/4	7/16
16	17 1/2	r	1/4	1/2	1 1/2	r	r
16	20	s	s	r	s	s	4
Bng o	36 5/8	s	s	24 1/2	s	s	r
60 1/4	40	s	s	21 1/4	s	s	r
60 1/4	43 3/8	16 1/2	r	r	r	r	1/8
60 1/4	46 5/8	13 3/8	r	r	r	r	r
60 1/4	50	9 7/8	r	11 1/4	r	r	1/4
60 1/4	53 3/8	6 7/8	7 1/8	8 1/4	r	r	r
60 1/4	56 5/8	3 5/8	4 1/4	5 1/4	r	r	1 3/8
60 1/4	60	r	2 3/8	3 5/8	r	1 3/4	r
Bois C	30	5 1/4	r	r	r	r	1/4
35 3/8	35	1/2	r	r	1/16	r	1 3/16
35 3/8	40	r	3/16	r	4 3/4	r	r
Brunos	15	5/8	1 1/16	1	r	3/4	r
C B S	170	35	s	r	r	s	r
204 7/8	175	30	s	r	r	s	r
204 7/8	185	r	r	r	r	3/8	r
204 7/8	190	14 1/4	r	r	r	7/8	r
204 7/8	200	4 1/2	8 5/8	r	r	2 7/8	r
204 7/8	210	1/16	4 1/4	7	5	7 3/4	r
CapCit	540	r	s	r	r	s	3 7/8
599 1/2	570	32	s	r	r	s	r
599 1/2	590	13	r	r	1/2	r	r
599 1/2	600	1/16	17 1/8	22 3/4	1/4	r	r
599 1/2	610	1/16	s	r	r	s	r
599 1/2	620	r	s	13 1/4	r	s	r
Coke	35	10	s	r	r	s	r
45	40	5	5 1/8	5 5/8	r	1/8	3/8
45	42 1/2	2 1/4	s	r	r	s	7/8
45	45	1/16	1 1/2	2 3/8	1/16	1 3/16	1 7/8
45	50	r	r	3/4	r	r	r
Colgat	60	5 3/4	r	6 1/2	r	r	r
66	65	9/16	2 3/8	3	1/16	1 1/4	r
66	70	r	r	15/16	r	r	r
Cmw Ed	30	r	r	r	r	r	1/4
33 1/4	35	r	r	1/4	r	2 1/2	r
33 1/4	40	s	s	1/16	s	s	r
C Data	20	r	r	7/8	1/2	r	r
Corng	45	2 3/8	r	r	r	r	r
47 5/8	50	r	r	r	2 3/4	r	r
Diebld	45	1/16	15/16	r	1/2	r	r
Edwrds	20	r	s	7 1/8	r	s	r
27 1/8	22 1/2	4 1/2	r	r	r	r	r
27 1/8	25	2	2 3/8	r	r	r	1/8
ForstL	40	4 1/8	5	r	r	r	r
43 5/8	45	r	1 9/16	r	r	r	r
43 5/8	50	r	1/4	r	r	r	r
GnCine	22 1/2	1/2	r	r	r	r	r
Gn Dyn	30	5 3/4	r	r	r	r	r
35 5/8	35	r	r	r	r	1	1 1/4
35 5/8	40	r	r	3/8	4 1/2	r	r
Gdrich	40	5 1/4	r	6 1/8	r	r	r
45 1/2	45	1/4	1 3/8	r	r	r	r
45 1/2	50	s	1/4	1/2	s	r	r
Harris	30	5	r	r	r	r	r
35	40	r	r	r	5	5 1/4	r
Hewlet	40	7 3/8	r	r	r	r	r
47 1/2	45	2 1/2	3 1/8	4	1/8	9/16	15/16
47 1/2	50	r	11/16	1 5/16	2 1/2	3	3 3/8
47 1/2	55	s	r	1/2	s	r	7 5/8
Honwll	85	14 3/8	s	r	r	s	3/8
98	90	8	r	r	r	r	r
98	95	2 7/8	5 5/8	7 1/8	r	1 1/4	r
98	100	1/16	2 3/8	4 1/8	1 3/4	r	4
98	105	r	1	2 1/8	r	r	r
Humana	35	10	s	r	r	s	r
45 1/8	40	5 1/4	r	r	r	r	1/4
45 1/8	45	3/16	1 1/4	r	1/16	1 1/8	r
InfoRs	10	r	s	6 1/2	r	s	r
16 3/8	15	1 1/2	1 3/4	r	r	r	r
16 3/8	17 1/2	r	r	3/4	r	r	r
In Flv	60	8 1/2	r	r	r	r	r
68 1/2	65	3 1/2	r	r	r	1/2	r
68 1/2	70	r	7/8	r	r	r	r
InLsFn	22 1/2	5	r	r	r	r	3/8
27 7/8	25	2 5/8	r	3 1/2	r	r	r
27 7/8	30	r	3/8	7/16	r	r	r
Limitd	35	13 1/2	s	r	r	s	r
48 3/4	40	8 1/2	r	9 1/2	r	r	r
48 3/4	45	4	4 5/8	5 1/4	r	11/16	1
48 3/4	50	r	1 1/2	r	1 1/4	2 9/16	r
Medtrn	60	r	s	r	r	s	1/2
79 1/4	65	14 1/4	s	r	r	s	r
79 1/4	70	9 1/2	r	r	r	r	r
79 1/4	75	r	5 5/8	r	r	13/16	r
79 1/4	80	1/16	r	r	1/2	r	r
Mobil	60	2 1/8	2 7/8	r	r	r	r
62 3/4	65	r	r	3/4	r	r	r
N Semi	5	2 5/8	r	2 3/4	r	r	1/16
7 5/8	7 1/2	1/16	7/16	11/16	r	3/8	r
7 5/8	10	r	r	1/8	2 3/8	r	r
Nthrop	17 1/2	1 3/4	2	r	r	r	r
18 7/8	20	r	5/8	7/8	r	r	r
Occi	25	1 7/8	2 1/16	2 3/8	r	1/16	1/8
27	30	r	1/16	3/16	3 1/8	r	r
27	35	s	s	1/16	s	s	r
Ogden	25	r	2	2 1/4	r	r	r
Pansph	12 1/2	r	2	2 1/2	r	r	3/8
14 3/8	15	r	r	13/16	r	r	r
14 3/8	17 1/2	r	s	5/16	r	s	r
Pegsus	10	r	1/2	5/8	r	r	r
9 7/8	12 1/2	r	r	3/8	r	r	r
I T T	50	r	r	9 1/2	r	r	r
58 3/4	55	3 7/8	4 1/4	5 1/8	r	3/8	3/4
58 3/4	60	1/16	15/16	2	1 3/16	r	2 3/8
58 3/4	65	r	r	3/4	r	r	r
K mart	30	6	r	r	r	r	r
35 3/4	35	13/16	1 1/4	2 1/4	r	7/16	1
35 3/4	40	r	r	3/8	4 3/8	r	r
LandsE	15	1 5/16	r	r	r	r	r
16 1/8	17 1/2	r	r	5/8	1 7/16	r	1 9/16
Litton	65	10 1/8	s	r	r	s	r
76 1/8	70	5 1/8	r	r	r	r	r
76 1/8	75	13/16	r	3 1/2	3/8	1 1/16	2
76 1/8	80	1/16	3/4	1 3/8	r	r	5 1/4
Loews	105	10 1/2	r	12 3/4	r	r	r
115 1/4	110	3 1/8	7 1/4	r	r	r	2 7/16
115 1/4	115	1/4	3 1/8	5 7/8	3/16	2 3/4	4
115 1/4	120	r	1 1/4	3 5/8	r	r	r
115 1/4	125	r	r	2	r	r	r
LongvF	12	3/8	s	r	s	s	s
12 1/4	13	r	s	11/16	7/16	s	r
MayDS	45	r	s	13	r	s	r
56 1/2	50	5 5/8	r	r	r	r	r
56 1/2	55	1 1/4	2	3 1/4	r	r	r
56 1/2	60	r	3/4	r	r	r	r
McCawC	30	r	r	r	r	1 11/16	r
Mc Don	25	10 1/2	s	r	r	s	r
35 1/2	30	5 1/2	r	6 1/4	r	r	3/16
35 1/2	35	3/8	1 3/8	2 5/16	1/16	11/16	1 1/16
35 1/2	40	r	3/16	7/16	r	r	r
N C R	60	7 5/8	s	r	r	s	r
67 3/4	65	2 1/2	3 3/4	5 1/4	r	3/4	1 5/8
67 3/4	70	r	1 1/8	r	2 1/4	3 3/8	r
NorSo	40	3 1/8	r	3 3/4	r	r	7/16
42 3/4	45	r	r	15/16	r	r	2 3/4
NorTel	20	9 1/2	s	r	r	s	r
29 5/8	22 1/2	7	s	r	r	s	r
29 5/8	25	4 3/4	r	5	r	r	1/4
29 5/8	30	r	7/8	1 1/2	r	r	r
Oracle	15	7 1/2	r	8	r	r	1/4
22 3/8	17 1/2	4 3/4	r	6	r	r	3/8
22 3/8	20	2 1/4	3	3 3/4	r	1/2	1
22 3/8	22 1/2	3/16	1 1/2	2 1/2	3/16	1 3/8	2
22 3/8	25	r	3/4	1 3/8	2 3/16	2 13/16	3 1/4
22 3/8	30	r	s	11/16	r	s	r
OutbdM	20	r	r	3/4	1	1 1/4	1 3/4
19 1/4	22 1/2	r	r	r	r	r	3 3/8
19 1/4	25	r	r	r	5 3/4	r	r
Pall	35	1/8	r	r	r	r	r
ParaCm	40	6 1/2	7 1/8	7 5/8	r	r	r
46 5/8	45	1 1/2	2 3/4	4	r	13/16	r
46 5/8	50	1/16	13/16	1 7/8	3 1/2	3 7/8	4 3/8
46 5/8	55	r	5/16	13/16	r	r	r
RalPur	80	13	r	r	r	r	r
93 7/8	85	8 7/8	[illegible]	r	r	r	1/2
93 7/8	90	3 5/8	4	5 1/2	r	r	1 3/4
93 7/8	95	r	1 3/8	2 1/2	r	r	r
93 7/8	100	s	r	1 1/8	s	r	r
Saatch	5	r	5/16	15/16	r	5/8	r
Schwab	15	3/8	r	1 5/8	1/16	r	r
SherW	35	3 1/4	r	r	r	r	r
39 5/8	40	r	r	r	r	2	r
SwAir	22 1/2	2 1/2	r	r	r	r	r
25	25	1/16	1	1 5/8	1/8	3/4	1 1/4
CmpAsc	12 1/2	3 3/4	r	4 1/4	r	r	r
15 3/4	15	7/8	1 3/8	2 1/4	r	r	7/8
15 3/4	17 1/2	r	3/16	1	1 1/2	1 1/2	r
CyprMn	22 1/2	r	7/8	r	r	5/8	r
22 1/4	25	r	3/16	r	r	2 1/8	r
22 1/4	30	r	1/16	1/4	r	r	r
Delta	70	9 3/8	10	r	r	r	r
79	75	4	5 3/8	r	r	5/8	2 1/8
79	80	1/8	1 3/4	r	13/16	r	r
79	85	s	7/16	r	s	r	r
DiaSrk	25	1/16	1 5/8	2 1/2	r	r	r
25 1/4	30	r	5/16	1 3/8	r	r	r
Dig Eq	75	11 1/4	r	r	r	r	r
87	80	6 1/4	r	r	r	r	r
Disney	105	27	r	r	r	r	r
131 3/4	110	21 7/8	r	r	r	r	r
131 3/4	130	1 3/8	6	r	r	r	r
Dryfus	35	5/8	r	r	3/16	r	r
35 5/8	40	r	r	5/8	r	r	r
EKodak	35	7	7 1/4	7 5/8	r	1/16	r
42	40	2	2 1/2	3 3/4	r	5/16	1 1/8
42	45	r	3/8	1 7/16	3	3 1/4	4
Eaton	55	r	7 3/4	r	r	r	r
62	60	r	r	r	r	7/8	1 5/8
62	65	r	5/8	r	r	r	r
Engelh	17 1/2	5 1/8	5	r	r	r	r
22 3/4	20	2 3/4	2 3/4	r	r	r	r
22 3/4	22 1/2	r	7/8	1 1/2	r	r	r
Enron	55	r	r	2 1/8	r	1 5/8	r
Everex	7 1/2	1 3/16	1 9/16	2	r	r	r
9 1/4	10	r	1/4	3/4	1 1/8	r	r
Exxon	40	8 1/8	r	r	r	r	r
48	45	2 13/16	3 5/8	4 1/4	r	3/16	11/16
48	50	r	5/16	1 1/16	2	2 1/8	r
FedExp	40	s	r	r	s	1/4	r
48 1/2	45	3 1/2	4 1/2	6	r	9/16	r
48 1/2	50	1/16	1 1/4	3	1 1/8	2 1/2	r
48 1/2	55	r	5/16	r	r	r	r
48 1/2	60	r	1/8	r	11 1/2	r	r
FstChi	25	7 3/8	r	r	r	r	r
32 3/8	30	2 3/8	r	r	r	r	r
32 3/8	35	r	r	1	r	r	3 1/4
Flntste	30	r	r	13 1/2	r	r	r
43 3/8	35	8	r	r	r	1/4	r
43 3/8	40	3 1/8	4 1/2	5 3/4	r	7/8	2 1/4
43 3/8	45	s	1 5/8	3 1/2	s	r	r
43 3/8	50	s	5/8	2 1/4	s	r	8 1/8
Fluor	35	s	r	r	s	1/16	r
47 3/4	40	8	7 3/4	r	r	r	r
47 3/4	45	2 1/2	3 5/8	r	r	1/2	1 1/2
47 3/4	50	r	1	2 5/8	r	2 7/8	r
GraphS	10	1/16	r	r	r	r	r
GrtWF	15	3 5/8	r	r	r	1/16	r
18 7/8	17 1/2	1 3/8	1 1/8	r	r	3/8	7/8
18 7/8	20	r	1/2	7/8	1 3/8	1 1/2	r
18 7/8	22 1/2	s	r	3/8	s	r	r
Grumm	15	1 1/8	1 1/4	r	r	r	3/4
Halbtn	40	7 1/4	r	r	r	r	r
48	45	2 7/8	3 1/8	4 3/4	r	r	1 1/4
48	50	r	5/8	2 1/4	2 1/8	3	r
48	55	r	r	r	7 3/4	r	r
Harsco	25	r	5/16	r	r	r	r
Hitachi	90	s	r	r	s	11/16	r

MOST ACTIVE OPTIONS

CHICAGO BOARD

		Sales	Last	Chg.	N.Y. Close
CALLS					
SP100	Jun345	75142	1 1/2	– 5/8	345.87
SP100	Jun340	27473	6 3/8	+ 1/8	345.87
SP100	Jun350	15919	1-16	– 1/4	345.87
SP100	Jul360	12920	1 1/2	– 1/2	345.87
SP100	Jul345	12116	8	– 1/8	345.87
PUTS					
SP100	Jun345	62686	1-16	– 1 1/8	345.87
SP100	Jun340	23485	1-16	– 1/4	345.87
SP100	Jun350	16009	3 1/2	– 7/8	345.87
SP100	Jul345	13810	4 3/4	– 7/8	345.87
SP100	Jul340	13738	3 1/4	– 5/8	345.87

AMERICAN

		Sales	Last	Chg.	N.Y. Close
CALLS					
MMIdx	Jun585	14181	1 1/8	– 3-16	586.14
Reebok	Oct20	7574	1 3/8	+ 3/8	18 5/8
MMIdx	Jun580	6060	6	+ 2 1/8	586.14
MMIdx	Jul620	5278	1	– 1/4	586.14
Disney	Jun130	5014	1 1/2	+ 7/8	131 3/4
PUTS					
MMIdx	Jun580	5434	1-16	– 1 5/8	586.14
MMIdx	Jun575	4619	1-16	– 1/2	586.14
Ph Mor	Jun45	3720	1 1/8	+ 5-16	44
MMIdx	Jun585	2609	1-16	–4 3-16	586.14
Apple	Jun40	2591	1/2	+ 1/4	39 1/2

PHILADELPHIA

		Sales	Last	Chg.	N.Y. Close
CALLS					
F N M	Jun40	1494	1 9-16	–1 1-16	41 5/8
Abbt L	Aug37 1/2	1180	2 5-16	– 1-16	38 5/8
F N M	Jul45	862	5/8	– 5-16	41 5/8
McGHil	Jul55	761	2 11-16	+ 7-16	56 3/8
Waste	Jun40	756	13-16	– 1-16	40 3/4
PUTS					
UniTel	Jul40	608	1 1/2	+ 1/2	39 7/8
F N M	Jul40	407	7/8	+ 3-16	41 5/8
SafKln	Jul35	400	11-16	+ 1-16	38 1/8
Abbt L	Aug37 1/2	315	1 1/4	+ 1/8	38 5/8
NwmtG	Jul40	303	3	– 1/2	38 1/4

PACIFIC

		Sales	Last	Chg.	N.Y. Close
CALLS					
Wendy	Sep7 1/2	3942	3/4	....	6 3/4
Hilton	Jun55	3333	1 5-16	+13-16	56 1/4
Compaq	Jun130	2947	1-16	– 5-16	128
Scher	Jun45	2550	1	– 7/8	45 7/8
Scher	Jul45	2378	1 7/8	– 1/8	45 7/8
PUTS					
Mc D D	Aug40	706	3	....	38 5/8
Hilton	Jul55	705	1 5-16	– 3-16	56 1/4
Compaq	Jul115	692	1 1/4	– 1/8	128
TCBY	Jul20	658	2 1/2	....	18 5/8
Compeq	Jul125	654	3 5/8	– 1/4	128

NEW YORK

		Sales	Last	Chg.	N.Y. Close
CALLS					
CSoup	Jul65	4299	2 7-16	....	60 5/8
CSoup	Jul60	2532	4	+ 3/8	60 5/8
ConFrt	Sep17 1/2	1182	1 1-16	– 1/2	16 1/4
QntmCp	Jun22 1/2	756	1-16	– 1-16	22 1/2
Chubb	Jul45	750	3 3/8	– 2 1/8	47 3/4
PUTS					
Chubb	Jul45	750	5-16	– 1-16	47 3/4
ConFrt	Jun17 1/2	432	1 1/8	+ 9-16	16 1/4
ConFrt	Sep20	405	4 1/8	+ 1/2	16 1/4
NY Idx	Aug200	220	5 1/2	+ 5/8	197.86
NY Idx	Jul200	216	4 1/4	+13-16	197.86

Figure 3.1. Options Table Example

for each of the three months in which Honeywell *calls* are traded, June, July, and August.

The letter *S*, as in the HON Jul 85 calls, indicates no such option exists. The letter *r*, as in HON Jul 90 calls, indicates that no transactions in that particular option took place on that day.

The final three columns show the closing premium value for each of the three months in which Hon *puts* are traded. Again, *S* means that option does not exist (Hon Jul 85 puts) and *r* indicates that no trade took place in this option on the day in question (Hon Jul 90 puts).

Two terms used frequently in the options area are *class* and *series.*

Class

A class of options consists of all options of the same type (put or call) covering the same underlying security. All Honeywell calls comprise a class of options. All Honeywell puts comprise a different class of options. All IBM calls make up a class. All General Motors puts are a class of option.

Series

A series of options is all options of the same class having both the same strike price and the same expiration month. In the one class of Honeywell calls, there is a number of different series as each call within that class has a different strike price and/or a different expiration month from any other option within the class. Each individual option is called a series. The total of all puts or calls on a particular stock makes up a class.

While looking at our options page, we can isolate examples of other familiar terms.

In the Money

An option is "in the money," if, based on the strike and market prices, it has an intrinsic value.

A call is "in the money" if the market price of the stock is higher than the strike price.

A put is "in the money" if the market price of the stock is lower than the strike price.

EXAMPLE: In the left-hand column of Figure 3.1, you will find CBS calls. If we look at the closing price of CBS stock we find it was 204⅞. The Jul 200 call is in the money. It has an intrinsic value of 4⅞ points. If you exercised the call, you could purchase CBS stock at $200 a share. The market value of 204⅞ would be higher than the strike price.

EXAMPLE: CBS JUL 210 Put

This put is in the money as it has an intrinsic value of 5⅛ points. If you owned this put, you could exercise and sell CBS stock at $210 a share. The stock could be purchased in the market for 204⅞ a share. That difference of 5⅛ points is the "in the money amount."

Notice that in the money does not necessarily mean that the option would be profitable at this point.

The CBS Jul 200 call is 4⅞ points in the money but the premium was 8⅝. The difference between intrinsic value and the actual premium represents the time value.

The Jul 210 put has an in the money value of 5⅛ points. But note that the premium on the put was 7¾.

The premium consists of

5⅛ Intrinsic value
2⅝ Time value
7¾ Total premium

Out of the Money

An option is "out of the money" if, based on the market and strike prices, there is no intrinsic value. From our options information we can note the following example of options that are out of the money.

EXAMPLE: Loews Jul 120 Call (center column)

As Loews stock closed at a price of 115¼, an option to purchase (call) the stock at 120 has no intrinsic value. Yet the premium for this call was 1¼ representing entirely time value. The call does not expire until July. A great deal can change during that time.

So the Loews July 120 Call is out of the money but it is not without value.

EXAMPLE: Colgate July 65 Put

Colgate stock closed at 66. As this put option allows the holder to sell the stock at 65 there is no intrinsic value. The premium for the option is 1¼ which represents time value only.

At the Money

An option is "at the money" if the market price of the stock and the strike price of the option are the same.

EXAMPLE: Coke Jul 45 Call (left column)

Coke stock closed at 45, which is the same as the strike price. The option is at the money. Again there is no intrinsic value and the 1½-point premium represents the time value.

OPTIONS DERIVATIVES

In simple terms, the options premium is determined by the three factors mentioned earlier, intrinsic value, time value, and volatility.

But there are other, more sophisticated tools used to measure the potential variations of options premiums. They are generally employed by professional options traders and may not be of interest to the individual investor, but a brief explanation of these terms adds to our overall knowledge.

These four tools are known as options derivatives. They are:

Delta

Gamma

Theta

Vega

Delta

An options' delta is used to measure the anticipated percentage of change in the premium in relation to a change in the price of the underlying security. If a particular call option had a delta of 60% we would expect the option premium to vary by 60% of the change in the underlying stock. If that stock rose 1 point, the option premium should rise approximately ⁶⁄₁₀ (60%) of 1 point.

Each series of options would have a different delta which could range from 0% to 100%.

If, for example, IBM stock were trading at 110 a share, an IBM Oct 80 put might have a delta factor of 0%. As this put is out of the money by a great amount, a change in the price of the stock may have no effect on this option's premium. However, with IBM trading at 110, an IBM Oct 80 call might have a delta factor of 100%. A rise in the stock of 1 point could increase the option premium by the same amount.

The IBM Oct 80 put is "deep out of the money." A price change on the stock might have no effect on the option.

The IBM Oct 80 call is "deep in the money." A rise in the

value of the underlying stock could have a major effect on the premium.

Gamma

Gamma measures the expected change in the delta factor of an option when the value of the price of the underlying security rises. If a particular option had a delta of 60% and a gamma of 5%, an increase of 1 point in the value of the stock would increase the delta factor by 5% from 60% to 65%. We would use the new delta to measure future price movement.

Theta

The theta derivative attempts to measure the erosion of an option's premium caused by the passage of time. We know that at expiration an option will have no time value and will be worth only the intrinsic value if, in fact, it has any. Theta is designed to predict the daily rate of erosion of the premium.

Assume an option has a premium of 3 and a theta of .06. Each day the premium should erode by .06. After one day it will decline to 2.94, the second day to 2.88, and so forth. Naturally other factors, such as changes in the value of the underlying stock will alter the premium. Theta is concerned only with the time value. Unfortunately, we cannot predict with accuracy changes in a stock's market value, but we can measure exactly the time remaining until expiration.

Vega

The first two options derivatives, delta and gamma, measure the effect on an option's premium due to changes in the value of the underlying stock. The third, theta, measures the decay caused by the passage of time.

The fourth derivative, vega, is concerned with the volatility factor of the underlying stock. We have pointed out that the volatility varies among different securities. Vega measures the amount by which the premium will rise when the volatility factor of the stock increases.

If, for example, XYZ stock has a volatility factor of 30% and the current premium is 3, a vega of .08 would indicate that the premium would increase to 3.08 if the volatility factor increased by 1% to 31%. As the stock becomes more volatile the changes in premium will increase in some proportion. Vega measures the sensitivity of the premium to these changes in volatility.

Delta, gamma, theta, and vega are very sophisticated tools for predicting changes in an option's premium. They merely take the three factors which determine a premium (price of the stock, passage of time, and volatility), and measure each in an exacting manner. The derivatives vary for each series of options.

For example, the derivative measures for a Honeywell Jul 90 call would differ greatly from those for a Honeywell Jul 100 call.

If Honeywell stock was trading at 98, the Jul 90 call would be in the money by 8 points. The Jul 100 call would be out of the money by 2 points. A 1 point rise in Honeywell stock to 99 would lead to an increase in the option premium by almost the same amount. For the Jul 90 call, it is now 9 points in the money. But the same 1-point rise might have little or no effect on the Jul 100 call. It is still 1 point out of the money.

If no further change in the price of the stock took place before expiration, each option would be worth its intrinsic value. For the Jul 90 call that would be 9 ($900), for the Jul 100 call the value at expiration would be zero.

While our study concentrates on options listed in exchanges, there are options that trade in the over-the-counter market. As stated, expiration months and strike prices are established by the exchange on which the options trade. If a client had a need for a put or call with a month or strike price not available on the exchanges, he might attempt to purchase it off the exchanges in the over-the-counter (OTC) market. It is also possible that the need might arise for an option on a security not listed on any of the exchanges. There are many thousands of stocks traded in the marketplace but only about 500 of them have exchange-listed options. For the others, the OTC market may provide an answer for the option-seeking investor.

Over-the-counter options are generally referred to as *conventional* options. The market is informal and is not very active, as many large brokerage firms prefer to limit their activities to exchange-traded products.

In some cases, over-the-counter options are used to enhance the features of a new offering of securities. This is generally done in conjunction with initial public offerings (IPOs) of low-priced speculative issues.

EXAMPLE: An underwriter is attempting to sell a new issue of one million shares of Golden Widget stock at $2 a share. This is the first time that stock of this company has been offered to the public. There is no current market for the shares.

Golden Widget has a very limited business history. The company has been in existence for only three months and its first widget has not been manufactured. There is also some question as to how great the market will be for golden widgets. In brief, potential investors are not anxious to pay $2 a share for a stock that may soon become worthless. In an effort to make the offering more attractive, the underwriter develops a unique strategy. For every 100 shares of Golden Widget purchased, the investor will also receive a put option entitling him to sell 100 shares of the stock at $1½ during the next six months.

The put option now limits the investor's loss over the next six months to 50 cents a share. If Golden Widget declines in value, or in fact becomes worthless, the investor can exercise his put and sell his position at $1½ a share. With the risk now reduced, investors may be willing to speculate on the future of this untested company.

Another enticement to buy Golden Widget is the use of calls on the stock. When purchasing shares at $2 each, the offering would include a call on the stock. For each 100 shares purchased, the investor can receive a call on 100 shares at $2½ a share, expiring in six months. Now, if Golden Widget becomes a roaring success and the stock rises to $5, each investor can exercise the calls and purchase additional stock at $2½. If need be, the underwriter could add both a put and a call to the package. Buy shares at $2 and receive a six-month put to sell at $1½ and a six-month call to buy at $2½. The possibilities are endless. But so are the risks.

When an investor purchases a listed option, put or call, performance is guaranteed by the Options Clearing Corporation. If an investor exercises a General Electric Corp. call he will receive his stock. Should the investor exercise a Texas Instruments put he will be paid the aggregate exercise price.

However over-the-counter options are generally guaranteed by some third party. If this third party is a major brokerage firm, such as Merrill Lynch or Morgan Stanley, the holder of the option can feel secure. But if the endorser of the option is an unknown entity, the contract may prove to be worthless. For example, if Golden Widget drops to 10 cents a share, the investor attempts to exercise his put at $1½ a share. But the party who granted the option has gone bankrupt, or has disappeared. The put cannot be exercised and the supposed protection to the investor proves to be a sham.

The value of owning a put or a call is entirely dependent on the ability of the writer to live up to the obligation assumed. With listed options, the risk of a failure to perform is negligible.

With over-the-counter options, a far greater chance of default exists. When buying an option, a privilege is received. It is incumbent on the buyer to know the condition of the party who sold him this privilege.

Since we are discussing over-the-counter options, we will take a brief look at their use in the bond markets. Bond dealers often employ put options to facilitate transactions. These trades can involve bonds of corporations, the U.S. Treasury, or municipalities, and they are often based on very large dollar amounts of securities.

For example, a dealer in municipal securities is attempting to sell one million face amount of State of California 8% bonds. The offering price for the bonds is 101. As bonds are priced as a percentage of $1,000, a price of 101 is equivalent to $1,010 per thousand or $1,010,000 for the entire block of bonds. The dealer is experiencing some difficulty in placing the bonds with his clients, so he decides to offer an added incentive.

He will give the buyer of the bonds a "put option." Under the terms of the put, the buyer will have the right to sell (put) the bonds to the dealer at any time during the next 30 days. Perhaps the price at which the bonds can be put will be somewhat below the original sales price. The customer's right to sell might be at a price of 100 ($1,000 per bond). Given this inducement, a large client, conceivably a commercial bank, purchases the securities. For the next 30 days the client has a maximum risk of $10 per bond or a total of $10,000. If the bonds are above a price of 100, the client will not exercise the put but the option has protected him against a substantial loss for a period of time. The risk to the dealer is that he may have to repurchase the securities, however, the securities will be at a price below that at which they were originally sold. Any profit made on the sale will provide the dealer with additional protection against loss in the event that the put is exercised against him.

An example of this is if he has a profit of ¾ of a point

($7.50) per bond on the original sale. If required to buy them back at 100, he would suffer no loss if he resold the securities at a price no lower than 99¼. The risk to the dealer is not eliminated but is considerably reduced. Dealers in securities, either stocks or bonds, are accustomed to taking risks. It is part of their business.

The use of put options in bond transactions is quite commonplace in today's markets. The example given above is not typical of the application of equity options. Rather, these are created by bond dealers to fit a particular trading situation. Such options are not traded on exchanges and therefore qualify as over-the-counter or conventional options.

In general, the discussion in this book is limited to exchange-listed options, but we would be remiss if we failed to demonstrate some of the other uses of these products.

CHAPTER 4

The Options Clearing Corporation

Although options trade on exchanges in much the same way as do stocks, the clearing and settlement of transactions is handled quite differently.

When a client purchases a stock there is a physical delivery of a certificate which is evidence of ownership of the shares. The certificate may be kept by the client or held by his broker for safekeeping. If at a later date the shares are sold, the certificate must be delivered to the buyer. It is then sent to a transfer agent, usually a bank, which changes the ownership and issues a new certificate. As you can easily see, this is an expensive and time-consuming process. If the certificate is lost, stolen, or destroyed further complications will arise.

These problems are not present in the trading of equity options, as no certificates are issued. All records of ownership and transfer are kept by a clearing organization called the Options Clearing Corporation (OCC). The entire process is computerized, allowing the industry to avoid the problems caused by physical certificates.

The OCC is jointly owned by the exchanges on which the options are listed. In addition to equity options, the OCC clears transactions in the other options products, stock indexes, foreign currencies, and U.S. Treasury securities.

To explain the process thoroughly, the journey of a hypothetical equity options transaction will be traced.

IBM stock is trading at $110 a share and client-A feels the price will rise. She calls her broker, Dean Witter, and enters the following order:

Buy 1 IBM Jan 110 Call @ Market

The instruction to buy at the market indicates she is willing to pay the best price that her broker can arrange.

But client-B is of the opposite opinion. He expects IBM stock to decline in price and enters the following order through his broker, Merrill Lynch:

Sell (write) 1 IBM Jan 110 Call – Premium 4

Client-B knows that if IBM stock declines as he anticipates, the call will not be exercised, and he will retain the $400 premium.

The brokers for the two clients meet on the floor of the CBOE and the following transaction occurs:

1 IBM JAN 110 Call – Premium 4

Buyer – Dean Witter Reynolds

Seller – Merrill Lynch

The following day this transaction will be recorded at the OCC. But no certificate will be issued. The books will be adjusted to add one IBM Jan 110 call to Dean Witter's previous position. If Dean Witter clients had been long a total of 173 of these calls before, the records would now show them long 174. Dean Witter's account at the OCC will also be debited the $400 premium.

The opposite entries are made in Merrill's account at the OCC. Its position in IBM Jan 110 calls will be reduced by one option, and it will be credited with the $400 premium.

Table 4.1 shows the adjustments that the computer will record.

The names of clients-A and -B who were the actual parties to this trade are not on record at the OCC, but their accounts at Dean Witter and Merrill Lynch will reflect the purchase and sale.

It is common practice in the securities industry to require a client to pay the premium for an options purchase no later than the day following the transaction. Although Federal Reserve regulations allow seven business days for payment, the OCC requires next-day payment. Dean Witter does not wish to use its own funds to pay for client-A's purchase, so next-day payment is generally demanded.

The simplicity of this trade when compared to a trade in a stock is evident. If client-B sold IBM stock rather than the call option, he would have to deliver the shares to Merrill Lynch. Merrill would then deliver to Dean Witter, perhaps through a clearinghouse, and receive payment. Dean Witter would then have to send the shares to a transfer agent to have a new certificate issued in the name of client-A. Not so in options. The

Table 4.1. Options Clearing Corporation: IBM Jan 110 Call

Dean Witter Reynolds	Merrill Lynch
+1	−1
−$400	+400

process is completely simplified. The computer does the work.

But the role of the OCC is far from over. We must now look at the method employed when an equity option is exercised.

If IBM stock rose to $125 a share, client-A might wish to exercise her call and purchase the shares at 110. At her instruction, Dean Witter would send an exercise notice to the OCC on 1 IBM Jan 110 Call. Although this option was originally purchased in a transaction with Merrill Lynch, it is entirely possible that some other firm will be called on to deliver the shares. The OCC consults its computers to determine how many firms have written an IBM Jan 110 Call. There may well be dozens of firms other than Merrill Lynch who are short this option. From this list the OCC selects one of the firms at random and notifies it that they have been exercised. Perhaps it may be Merrill, but the other firms have an equal chance of being selected. The selection is done totally at random. Perhaps this exercise notice will be assigned to Paine Webber. It will be told to deliver 100 shares of IBM at $110 a share to Dean Witter. Paine Webber will have five business days to complete the delivery as this is the normal period for settling transactions in the securities industry. But Paine Webber may have 100 or more different clients who have written this call. Who gets exercised? Paine Webber can do as the OCC did, and make a selection at random. But it has another choice. It may use a system known as FIFO (First in, first out). Whichever Paine Webber client wrote the IBM Jan 110 Call first will be exercised first. The second writer gets the second exercise and so forth. A brokerage firm can use either system, random selection or FIFO, as long as it is consistent. Perhaps Paine Webber assigns the notice against John Jones. He may own 100 IBM shares, so his broker will simply deliver them to Dean Witter. But suppose Jones wrote the call uncovered. In this case, he will have to purchase or borrow the shares to make delivery. Once a call is exercised against you, the shares must be delivered.

Table 4.2. Options Clearing Corporation: IBM Jan 110 Call

Original Purchaser	Original Writer
Dean Witter Reynolds	Merrill Lynch
	Exercised against
	Paine Webber
	Assigned notice
	Client: J. Jones

A careful study of the monthly statement sent to you by your broker will indicate which method his firm employs in exercising options.

Naturally if IBM stock continues to trade above $110 a share, all persons who wrote IBM Jan 110 calls will be exercised. But we cannot predict the future. If IBM declines to 105 before expiration in January, any outstanding calls will expire unexercised. Table 4.2 shows an example of this process.

Although the purchaser of a put or call has the right to exercise at any time prior to expiration, options are seldom exercised until the expiration date. In the period of time prior to expiration, the client would most likely find it more profitable to sell the option rather than exercise it. The premium is in part made up of time values.

At expiration all of the time value has eroded but prior to expiration the premium may reflect the remaining time.

For example:

MCI Jan 50 Put

Market price of MCI - 47¾

The intrinsic (in the money) value of this put is 2¼ points. It gives the holder the right to sell the stock at $50 a share while the market price is only $47 and ¾ a share.

If this option were due to expire tomorrow the premium would be 2¼. That's all it's worth. It has intrinsic value but has no time left.

If there were still a month to go before expiration, however, the premium might be 3½. To the 2¼ points of intrinsic value 1¼ points of time value can be added. If an owner of this put wished to eliminate his position at this time he would be wiser to sell the option than to exercise it.

In fact most individual investors who purchase options never intend to exercise them. They hope to purchase the option at one price and sell it later at a higher price much as they attempt to do in trading stock. But dealing in options presents a problem that does not exist in stocks. There is a provision in options trading known as *automatic exercise* which clients must understand. This provision states that the OCC will automatically exercise any equity option that is ¾ of a point or more in the money at expiration.

As we will explore later in this chapter, equity options expire on a Saturday. Based on the closing price of the underlying stocks on the previous Friday, an option with an intrinsic value of ¾ of a point or more will be automatically exercised. This could lead to a situation that the client has not bargained for.

A client purchases:

10 Teledyne Jan 360 Calls – Premium 3

This client thought Teledyne stock would rise so she paid $3,000 to purchase 10 calls on the stock. Her intent was to sell the calls, perhaps at 5, when the stock went up, and make enough money for a little vacation. At no time did she intend to exercise the calls. She just wanted to buy them and sell them at a profit. But things did not work out as she had hoped, and Teledyne did not rise in value. In fact, on Thursday, two days before the Saturday expiration, the stock was trading at 359 and the 360 calls had no intrinsic value. She had accepted the fact that the hoped-for vacation would have to be postponed. But markets are unpredictable. Late Friday afternoon, the market rallied and Teledyne stock rose and closed at 360¾. Her calls would now be automatically exercised as they ended their life ¾ of a point in the money. On Monday her broker would be telephoning to ask her to send in $360,000 to pay for the purchase of 1,000 shares of Teledyne at $360 a share. Needless to say this might present a problem. To make matters worse, the market went down on Monday, and Teledyne was now worth $357 a share. This experience might lead our client to pursue some hobby that is less risky than options, perhaps fighting oil well fires.

This example is not exaggerated. It can and does happen if the client is unaware of the automatic exercise. If you do not wish to be caught in this situation, you must watch the market closely. Sell the option before expiration. You may not receive a large amount, but you will eliminate the possibility of having it exercised.

KEY TIMES AND DATES

The options exchanges establish the trading regulation and terms of exercise. Certain times and dates are important to know. The following information is stated in Eastern Standard Time. Make the necessary adjustment if you reside in a different time zone.

Options Expiration

Equity options expire at 11:59 PM on the Saturday following the third Friday of the stated expiration month. This is usually the third Saturday of the month but *not* always. If the first day of the month falls on a Saturday, the Saturday following the third Friday will be the fourth Saturday of that month. (Confusing isn't it?)

Market Hours

Trading in equity options is conducted from 9:30 AM to 4:10 PM each business day. The one exception is on the last trading day prior to expiration (the third Friday of the month) when trading ceases at 4 PM.

Exercise Notices

Other than on the last trading day for each month, exercise notices may be presented to the OCC between 10 AM and 4:30 PM. On the last trading day (that third Friday again), exercise notices will be accepted until 5:30 PM.

Premium Due at Options Clearing Corporation

Premiums due for the purchase of options are made to the OCC no later than 10 AM on the business day following the trade. This payment is made by the firm that handled the purchase order and is then charged to the client.

ENTERING ORDERS FOR EQUITY OPTIONS

When a client enters an order to purchase, sell long, or sell short an equity option, the firm handling the order transmits it to the exchange floor for execution. A record of the order is kept in the broker's office which contains the following information:

Buy or sell

Number of contracts

Underlying security

Expiration month

Strike price

Premium limit (if any)

Type (put or call)

Long or short (if sell)

Covered or uncovered (if short)

Identification of client

In addition the order must identify if this represents an *opening* or *closing* transaction. An *opening* transaction is one which initiates a position or increases a current position. A *closing* transaction is one which eliminates or reduces a current position.

Client Brown has studied the market and has determined that Pepsi stock is about to go up. He has no existing position but decides to purchase a call on the stock. He enters the following order:

Buy 1 Pepsi Jan 60 Call – Premium 3¼

As Brown has no position and is purchasing the contract, the order would be marked opening purchase.

Client Smith is of the opposite opinion. She feels Pepsi is due for a drop in price. She does not have a current position in Pepsi but decides to write a call on the stock. If Pepsi declines, she will keep the premium. She enters the following order:

Sell 1 Pepsi Jan 60 Call – Premium 3¼

This order is marked opening sale as she is initiating her position in this option.

Both Brown and Smith were entering orders that were opening transactions. One by purchasing, the other by selling.

The brokers for each client meet on the floor of the CBOE and a transaction takes place. Brown buys and Smith sells:

1 Pepsi Jan 60 Call – Premium 3¼

A few weeks later Brown is a happy man as Pepsi stock has risen in price. With this increase the premium on his call has risen to 5¼. He decides to sell the option. The order reads:

Sell 1 Pepsi Jan 60 Call – Premium 5¼

As he is eliminating his position, this is a closing sale. He bought at 3¼ and sold at 5¼. He has taken his profit and closed out his position.

But time proves Ms. Smith to be correct as well. Later Pepsi stock falls in price and the option premium declines to 1. She enters an order:

Buy 1 Pepsi Jan 60 Call – Premium 1

She sold at 3¼, she is repurchasing at 1 for a profit of 2¼ points. She has closed out her position by buying the option.

All orders are either opening or closing transactions and must be noted as such. In our example, the opening trades initiated position. If one adds to an existing position it is also considered an opening. Closing can be the elimination of a position or the reduction of a current one.

POSITION LIMITS AND EXERCISE LIMITS

As we have seen, options on equity securities are not created by the corporations that issue the underlying stock. They are created by people who write the contract in exchange for a premium. Therefore, there is no limit to the number of options that may be created for any corporation's stock. It is conceivable that the options could represent more shares than actually exist. Perhaps XYZ Corp. has 10 million shares of stock outstanding. It is possible that writers could create 150,000 call contracts on the company's stock. As each call represents 100 shares, the 150,000 contracts would represent 15 million shares of XYZ while only 10 million shares are in existence. Consider the chaos that would result if all of these calls were exercised. This is a radical and unlikely possibility, but let's look at one situation that might well occur. A group of market players wish to force up the price of a stock. They purchase, perhaps over a period of time, 20,000 calls representing 2 million shares of the underlying security. At some point, they exercise all of the call contracts. Without doubt many of the contracts will be exercised against uncovered writers who would be forced to purchase the stock in the open market to make delivery. The pressure of these orders would no doubt lead to a large increase in the stock's price and perhaps a large profit to our group that exercised the calls. They might now be able to sell a position that they had taken in the stock much earlier at the currently inflated price.

As a deterrent to this type of activity the Securities and Exchange Commission (SEC) has approved a limit on the size of a position in options that may be held. In brief the rule states:

> *No person or group acting in concert may have a position exceeding 8,000 options contracts on the same underlying security on the same side of the market.*

A person is any entity such as an individual, a corporation, a partnership, or trust. A group "acting in concert" would be defined as any group of persons who have agreed to the same pattern of trading or whose accounts are handled and controlled by the same advisor. We have discussed the sides of the market earlier. There are two sides, the upside and the downside.

Upside	Downside
Long calls	Long puts
Short puts	Short calls

No options position covering the same security, such as General Electric, can exceed 8,000 contracts on either of these sides. For example, the following positions would not violate this rule.

General Electric

Upside		Downside	
Long calls	5,000 contracts	Long puts	5,000 contracts
Short puts	3,000 contracts	Short calls	3,000 contracts
Total	8,000 contracts	Total	8,000 contracts

Although the total position is 16,000 contracts, neither side exceeds the allowable limit of 8,000. After all, the price of General Electric stock cannot be going up and down at the same time, so only one of these sides will be increasing in value at any given time.

The following position *does* violate the limits.

General Electric

Upside		Downside	
Long calls	5,000 contracts	Long puts	3,000 contracts
Short puts	5,000 contracts	Short calls	3,000 contracts
Total	10,000 contracts	Total	6,000 contracts

Again, the total position is only 16,000 contracts, but this time 10,000 are on one side—the upside. This is in violation of the limit.

The 8,000 contract limit applies to the most active stocks. For those that are less active in their trading, the limit declines to 5,500 or even 3,000 contracts per side. But the maximum in all cases is 8,000 contracts. The position limit has been changed many times since 1973 and most probably will be changed again as conditions warrant.

EXERCISE LIMITS

If a group wished to avoid the position limits, it might come up with this idea: On Monday it buys 8,000 calls on XYZ stock and exercises them Tuesday morning; on Tuesday afternoon it buys 8,000 more XYZ calls and exercises them on Wednesday morning. The group does this each day and exerts continuous pressure on XYZ stock. The group has not violated its position limits since its position did not exceed 8,000 contracts at any time.

But there is *another* rule that states that no person or group acting in concert can exercise more than 8,000 contracts covering the same underlying security in any five consecutive business days. So having exercised 8,000 XYZ calls on Tuesday morning, this group could not exercise any additional XYZ options until the following Tuesday.

As was the case with position limits, the 8,000-contract exercise limit is for the most active stocks. That limit declines to 5,500 or 3,000 contracts on stocks with less active trading volume.

The position and exercise limits are rarely a problem for the individual investor. After all, 8,000 contracts represent 800,000 shares of stock. Few individuals trade in that volume. But institutions with large holdings often write covered calls to increase income. These limits could affect their ability to write against an entire position.

A large investment company may own 500,000 shares of

American Telephone common stock. The stock was purchased sometime earlier at an average cost of $25 a share. The current price is $42 a share, thus the position has been very rewarding. The investment company's portfolio manager does not see any radical change in the price in the coming months and takes action to increase the income on the portfolio. At this time, AT&T Sep 45 calls are trading at a premium of 2½. The portfolio manager sells (writes) 5,000 covered calls at this price. The gross proceeds of the sale is $1,250,000 (5,000 options sold at $250 per contract). This money is added to the portfolio value and is available for future investment. If American Telephone stock does not rise above $45 a share between the time of the sale and the September expiration, the calls will not be exercised and the premium received will become a bonus. Of course, if American Telephone rises above $45 during the life of the option, the contracts will be exercised and the shares will be delivered. However, this is far from a disastrous result. The investment company receives the exercise price of $45, in addition, it had received earlier a premium of 2½ points a share. The actual sale price of the stock is $47½. As the investment company bought the stock at $25, the profit on the position is most satisfactory.

In this example, the sale of the 5,000 calls did not violate the position limit. However, if the investment company owned 1 million shares, it would not be permitted to write against the entire position. A long position of 1 million shares would facilitate the writing of 10,000 covered call options. This would exceed the permissible limit. Only 8,000 contracts could be written in this situation.

It should be noted that there are situations in which a person can have a position exceeding 8,000 contracts covering the same security on the same side of the market without violating the allowable limits. This would occur when the stock of the underlying company was the subject of a stock split.

For example, a client owns 6,000 Monsanto Chemical Nov 80 Puts. Monsanto announces its intention to split its stock 2 for 1. Each holder of 100 shares of Monsanto will now own 200 shares of stock. Naturally, the price of the stock will decline initially to reflect this increase in the outstanding price. If the price prior to the 2-for-1 split was $80 a share it would probably drop to about $40 a share after the split. When such an action occurs, it is necessary to make adjustments in the terms of outstanding options. In the case of a 2-for-1 split, the number of contracts will be doubled and the exercise price will be cut in half. (A complete discussion of this process can be found in Chapter 5.)

Therefore a holding of:

6,000 Monsanto Nov 80 Puts

will be adjusted to:

12,000 Monsanto Nov 40 Puts

This position of 12,000 contracts greatly exceeds the permissible maximum of 8,000. But no violation has occurred. The client did not create the position in excess of the allowable amount. It resulted from an action by the company over which the client had no control—the stock split. The client can retain this position, if so desired, until expiration of the options in November. Once the expiration of these contracts takes place, the usual limit of 8,000 will again apply.

Cash Dividends, Stock Dividends and Stock Splits

Most of the underlying stocks that equity options represent pay dividends to their shareholders. These payments are generally made on a quarterly basis. When a corporation declares a dividend, it establishes what is called the record date. In order to be entitled to the forthcoming dividend, you must be recorded on the books of the company as the owner of the stock on that date.

Using the calendar in Table 5.1 let us assume that General Motors declared a dividend of 75 cents a share to holders of record March 15.

The 75 cents a share will be paid only to the owners on the record on that day.

Table 5.1. Record Date: March

S	M	T	W	T	F	S
			1	2	3	4
5	6	7	8	9	10	11
12	13	14	(15)	16	17	18
19	20	21	22	23	24	25
26	27	28	29	30	31	

In the securities industry, a normal transaction, called a regular way trade, requires five business days to complete. If there are no holidays, five business days is one week. Therefore, to be eligible for this dividend, the latest date on which you could purchase General Motors shares would be Wednesday, March 8. That transaction would settle five business days later on March 15.

Had you purchased one day later on Thursday, March 9, it would be too late to receive the 75 cents a share dividend. That trade would settle one week later, on Thursday, March 16, the day after the record date.

In the language of securities, the fourth business day prior to the record date is called the "ex-dividend" date (as in "without" dividend). In our example, Thursday, March 9, is the ex-dividend date for the dividend payment by General Motors (see Table 5.2).

March 8 was the last date on which a purchase could be made in time to receive the dividend.

These dates are important for those who deal in equity options. If you own a call, you do not own the stock, just the privilege to purchase the shares. If you owned a call on General Motors and wished to receive the dividend, you would have to exercise prior to the ex-dividend date. The date of exercise is similar to the trade date for the purchase of stock. Just as you must purchase the stock at least five business days prior to the record date, you must exercise your call no later than that date

Table 5.2. Ex-Dividend Date: March

S	M	T	W	T	F	S
			1	2	3	4
5	6	7	8	⑨	10	11
12	13	14	15	16	17	18
19	20	21	22	23	24	25
26	27	28	29	30	31	

to be entitled to payment. A General Motors call exercised on March 8 would enable the holder to receive the dividend. If exercised on March 9 your call would be too late. General Motors' stock is ex-dividend on that date.

Suppose, however, you owned 100 shares of General Motors' stock and to protect your position, you purchased a General Motors put. On March 8, you exercised the put. In effect you have sold your stock on that date and will not receive the dividend. The party who was exercised against buys the stock on March 8, and she gets the dividend. Had you waited one day and exercised on March 9, the ex-dividend date, the dividend would have been yours.

To compensate for the loss of the dividend, the price of the stock usually declines on the ex-date. General Motors' stock might have been $48 a share on March 8. On March 9, it would probably begin trading at about $47¼.

Payment of cash dividends by a corporation *do not* affect the terms of an options contract. When a contract is exercised, however, the cash dividend may become a factor.

STOCK SPLITS AND STOCK DIVIDENDS

While cash dividends do not affect the terms of a listed options contract, stock splits and stock dividends by corporations require major adjustments.

If IBM stock was trading at $110 a share and announced a

2-for-1 split, the price of the shares would decline on the split date to about $55 or half the pre-split price. There are now twice as many shares outstanding, as each holder of shares will now receive an equal number of new shares. If you had owned 100 shares, you now own 200 shares. If a person owned an IBM Jun 110 call, he certainly would not be happy if the stock was now only 55. So we adjust the contract terms.

Similarly, if MMM stock, trading at $75 a share, declared a 30% stock dividend, each stockholder would receive 30% more shares. If he owned 100 shares, the company would send him 30 more. Now he owns 130 shares. But, again, the price of the stock will reflect the existence of these additional shares. Initially the price would decline from $75 to approximately $57⅝ per share ($75 divided by 130 shares).

If you had written an MMM Jan 75 put, you would have a problem if we did not alter the terms. The stock is now $57⅝, and the holder of the put would certainly exercise it against you at $75. So changes must be made.

There are two possible adjustments to stock splits and stock dividends. Some splits and dividends result in *round lot* holdings. Round lots are multiples of 100 shares. So if UAL split 4 for 1, the holder of 100 shares would now own 400 shares.

If MMM paid a 100% stock dividend, a 100-share holding would become 200 shares.

In round lots our adjustments are quite simple. We just increase the number of contracts in the same ratio as the split or dividend and reduce the strike price inversely:

EXAMPLE: UAL splits its stock 4 for 1:
    1 UAL Nov 280 Call becomes
    4 UAL Nov 70 Calls

We increase the number of calls from 1 to 4, which is the

same ratio as the split. We then divided the old strike price (280) by the split ratio (4) to arrive at the new strike price (70).

The amount of the money involved in either case is the same.

1 UAL Nov 280 Call represents 100 shares at $280 a share or $28,000.

4 UAL Nov 70 Calls represent 400 shares at $70 a share or $28,000.

These adjustments are made to all UAL options—both puts and calls. The new terms are now in tune with current market conditions.

EXAMPLE: MMM declares a 100% stock dividend.
1 MMM Jan 75 Put becomes
2 MMM Jan 37½ Puts

The number of contracts was doubled as was the number of outstanding shares, and the old strike price was divided by 2 in order to determine the new strike price.

Again the aggregate exercise price is the same; 100 shares at $75 equals $7,500. Two hundred shares at $37½ equals $7,500.

In this we have arrived at a strike price that is not usual. Most strike prices are set at intervals of 5 points. But in situations such as this, exceptions are made. When these contracts expire in January, they will not be renewed with the 37½ strike price, but until then the change is necessary in the interest of fairness.

In other cases splits and stock dividends result in an *odd number* of shares. An *odd lot* is considered to be an amount from 1 to 99 shares. In this case, our adjustment will be handled differently. The OCC will not issue new contracts representing odd lot amounts. They will simply increase the number of shares in the current contract to reflect the change.

EXAMPLE: UAL splits its stock 3 for 2

In this case, the holder of 100 shares would now own 150 shares. Thus, a 3 for 2 split is 300 for 200, and 100 shares would become 150 shares.

The option holder will not be given a second contract for 50 shares. We will simply increase the number of shares in the current contract and adjust the strike price accordingly.

1 (100 shares) UAL Nov 280 Call becomes
1 (150 shares) UAL Nov 93⅜ Call

The holder still owns one contract, but it now represents 150 shares of UAL stock. To determine the new strike price we divide the aggregate exercise value ($28,000) by the new number of shares (150).

$$\frac{\$28,000}{150} = 93.333$$

We cannot deal in decimal places so we round the decimal .333 to the nearest value of ⅛ of a point, which is .375 or ⅜. The total dollars are not exactly the same but are as close as we can get.

EXAMPLE: MMM pays a 30% stock dividend
1 (100 shares) MMM Jan 75 Put becomes
1 (130 shares) MMM Jan 57¾ Put

Again, the number of contracts does not change. But now the contract represents 130 shares of MMM stock. To determine the new strike price, we divide the aggregate exercise value of $7,500 by the new number of shares (130).

$$\frac{\$7,500}{130} = 57.692$$

We don't use decimal points in our trading so we round .692 to the nearest ⅛ of a point which would be .75 or ¾.

Again, the total dollars involved are not the same as in the original contract but the figure is very close.

When adjustments such as these occur they affect the total premium paid or received in future trading. Remember that the premium is measured by the number of shares in the contract.

If the holder of the UAL Nov 93⅜ call sold the option for a premium of 3 he would receive $450. The $3 premium is for each of the 150 shares now represented by this contract.

A buyer of the MMM Jan 57¾ put at a premium of 4 would pay $520. The contract is for 130 shares at a premium of $4 each.

The necessary adjustments to the terms of equity options contracts necessitated by stock splits and stock dividends do not cause any great operational problems. As there are no certificates used in options, only the OCC computer records the change. If you actually owned shares of the underlying stock, the corporation would have to send you the additional shares.

In addition to cash dividends, stock dividends, and stock splits, corporations often reward their stockholders with other forms of payment. If there are options based on these corporations' shares, it is often necessary to adjust the terms of the contracts to reflect these events. One such possibility is known as a "spin-off." In this situation, a corporation may own all of the stock of some other corporation. For some reason, perhaps a tax benefit, the owner of the shares elects to give the shares to its own stockholders.

As an example, assume that the ABC Corporation owns all of the stock of the CBA Corporation. ABC announces its intention to spin-off CBA's shares to its stockholders. The terms call for one share of CBA to be distributed for each share of ABC currently owned. Thus the holder of 100 shares of ABC will continue to own these shares but in addition will now own 100 shares of CBA. The total value of the ABC stockholder's holdings may not change but the components of that value will be altered. Perhaps, prior to the spin-off, ABC was valued at $40 a share. After this event, it may decline to $30 but the shares of CBA may have a market value of $10 a share.

From a standpoint of total worth, the two positions are the same:

Prior to spin-off	100	ABC	@	$40	=	$4,000
Subsequent to spin-off	100	ABC	@	$30	=	$3,000
	100	CBA	@	$10	=	$1,000
				Total		$4,000

But suppose there were outstanding options on ABC stock. The value of these contracts was based on a market value of $40; because that value has been reduced to $30 by an event other than normal market activity, some adjustment must be made. There is more than one way in which the situation can be handled and the final decision will be made by the exchanges on which the options are traded and by the Options Clearing Corporation.

For example, in the above-mentioned situation regarding ABC options, two possibilities exist. First, the exercise price on all outstanding options could be reduced to reflect the spin-off. If the value of CBA stock was in fact determined to be $10 a share, the strike price on ABC puts and calls would be reduced by that amount.

If ABC had outstanding options with strike prices of 35, 40, 45, and 50, they would be changed to 25, 30, 35, and 40, respectively. The number of shares represented by each option would remain 100, but the exercise price would be revised.

It would be unfair otherwise. Suppose you owned an ABC Nov 40 put prior to the spin-off. As the stock was then trading at $40 a share, the option had no intrinsic value. It was said to be at the money. Subsequent to the spin-off, ABC's stock value declined to $30 a share. Suddenly the Nov 40 put was 10 points in the money. If no adjustment is made, the owner of the put will be quite pleased. But what of the owner of an ABC Jul 35 call? With the stock at $40, his option to purchase at 35 had an intrinsic value of 5 points. Now as the stock is at $30, a call with a strike price of 35 is out of the money.

If the decline in price had occurred due to normal market activity, no adjustment would be made. Anyone who deals in options must bear that market risk. However, in this case, it was an outside event that led to the decline. For the sake of fairness, an adjustment will be made.

An equitable solution could also be found by leaving the exercise price unchanged but revising the terms of the settlement. All ABC options, both puts and calls, might now require the delivery of 100 shares of ABC *and* 100 shares of CBA. As the value of the two securities should be roughly the same as that of ABC alone prior to the spin-off, the option's positions would need no further adjustment. These cases are treated individually as the need arises but a solution that is fair to all parties will be found.

Another event that may cause an adjustment in the terms of equity options contracts is the issuance of "pre-emptive" rights. These rights give holders of a corporation's stock the privilege of purchasing additional shares. The price at which the new shares may be bought, the subscription price, is generally lower than the current market value of the shares. This is done as an inducement to the holders to subscribe to the shares. In most cases, these rights will have a value representing the discount at which the new shares can be purchased.

Suppose that the Public Service Electric & Gas Co. wishes

to raise additional capital by selling new shares of common stock. It might, of course, offer these shares in the market but it could also elect to offer them to its current shareholders through pre-emptive rights. In many cases, the company has no choice. The corporate charter may require that new shares first be offered to the stockholders. This prevents an owner from having his position diluted through an increase in the number of outstanding shares. Thus Public Service Electric & Gas (usually referred to as PEG) makes the following offer.

Each shareholder may purchase one new share of stock for each five shares currently held at a price of $20 a share. The current market price of PEG stock is $26 a share. This price of $26 represents a $6 a share premium over the subscription price.

Market price	$26
Subscription price	20
Premium	$ 6

In time, the rights will begin to be traded in the market and a value for each right will be determinable. Although the premium is $6, it requires five rights to purchase each share, so the approximate value of each right is $1.20.

Premium $6 Divided by 5 = $1.20

Owners or writers of options do not receive pre-emptive rights. Yet, the value of the right represents a corresponding loss of value of the underlying stock. When the rights are exercised, and they will be if a premium exists, there will be additional shares outstanding. This will dilute the earnings per share and increase the dollar amount of dividends to be paid by the corporation. The money received from the sale of the new shares will naturally be employed by the corporation and may offset some of the negative factors caused by the dilution. But the immediate value of the stock is reduced by the value of the pre-emptive rights. In most cases, the strike price of the options will be reduced by that same value. If, as in our example, the value of the rights is $1.20, a reduction of perhaps 1¼ points will be made. In listed options we only deal in variations of ⅛ of a point or multiples thereof. Thus a reduction of exactly $1.20 would not be workable. The final decision rests with the exchanges and the OCC but perhaps the following would occur:

PEG Feb 25 Call becomes PEG Feb 23¾ Call

PEG Jun 30 Put becomes PEG Jun 28¾ Put

If the value of the right is minimal there will most likely be no adjustment made. A value of 5 cents a right might well be ignored and all exercise prices would remain the same. Again, judgments are made on a case-by-case basis to best serve the interest of those who have option positions.

Earlier, we made brief mention of over-the-counter options which are referred to as conventional options. These options are adjusted in the same manner as exchange-traded options with regard to stock splits, stock dividends, spin-offs, and pre-emptive rights.

However, there is one difference. While listed options make no adjustment for cash dividends, conventional options do. The strike price is reduced by the exact amount of any cash dividend. If ABC Corporation paid a cash dividend of $2.50 a share, an ABC Oct 35 put would become an ABC Oct 32½ put.

These adjustments for cash dividends on over-the-counter options are made using the exact amount of the dividend. No rounding up or down to the nearest value of ⅛ is applied. If ABC paid a cash dividend of $2.09, the Oct 35 put would be adjusted to an ABC Oct 32.91 strike price.

As these changes in exercise prices affect the value of options, they must be completely understood by all investors who utilize the product.

ABC paid a cash dividend of $2.09, the Oct 35 Put would be adjusted to an ABC Oct 32.91 strike price.

Equity Options Strategies

We have looked at the basic uses of put and call options. They can be used to protect positions and to speculate on the price movement of the underlying security. Investors who think or fear that the market in a particular stock will rise can purchase calls or write puts. If a declining market is their concern they can take the opposite position and buy put options or write call options.

Equity options provide the opportunity to create other more-advanced strategies. These are not suitable for all investors but can be used to implement market techniques that otherwise could not be achieved using the underlying stocks.

STRADDLES

A *straddle* consists of both a put and a call on the same security with the same strike price and expiration month.

Note that a straddle consists of two options that are identical in every detail except that one is a put and the other is a call.

A client can use a straddle in one of two ways—a *long straddle*, or a *short straddle*.

In a *long straddle* the client would *purchase* the put and the call. In a *short straddle* she would *write* both the put and the call. We will look at these positions separately and learn the reasoning behind each position as well as the potential risks and rewards.

Long Straddle

An investor has made a careful study of the trading pattern of Walt Disney stock. She feels that the stock is about to experience a major move in price. But she is not sure in which direction, up or down, this price move will occur. A long straddle might enable her to implement her theory.

She might "put on" the following long straddle (options people use the term "put on" not buy.)

Buy 1 Disney Dec 130 Call – Premium 10

Buy 1 Disney Dec 130 Put – Premium 6½

With this position she will participate in any movement in Disney stock be it up or down. If the stock rises, the value of the call will increase. If it falls, the put becomes more valuable. She has, however, paid a total of 16½ points in premium to establish the position. The call premium was 10 ($1,000), and the put cost was 6½ ($650).

Before our client can show a profit, she must recapture the 16½ points of premium. Therefore, at expiration in December, Disney stock must be at 146½ or at 113½ for her to break-even on this straddle. If Disney is at 146½, she could exercise her call at 130, and sell the stock at 146½. The profit of 16½ points is equal to the total premium payment.

If at expiration Disney stock is down to 113½, she could purchase stock at that price and exercise her put, selling the stock at 130. Again a profit of 16½ points, which offsets her premium cost.

Any price above 146½ or below 113½ would represent a profit. Technically the profit potential is unlimited as her call allows her to buy stock at 130. It could rise to any possible point above that price.

In no case can she lose more than 16½ points. We have stated this fact before, but it is worth repeating. *The buyer of options cannot lose more than the premium paid to establish the position.* We can look at the possibilities of this straddle in Figure 6.1.

It is possible, though unlikely, that Disney stock could become worthless. As this client can put (sell) the stock at 130

Figure 6.1. Buy 1 Disney Dec 130 Call – Premium 10
Buy 1 Disney Dec 130 Put – Premium 6½

↑↓	Unlimited potential profit
146 1/2 Break-even (call)	
↑↓	Potential loss of up to 16 1/2 points
130 Strike price	
↑↓	Potential loss of up to 16 1/2 points
113 1/2 Break-even (put)	
↑↓	Potential profit of 113 1/2 points

she would have a profit of 113½ points. She could acquire the shares at no cost and sell at 130. From this we subtract the 16½ points of premium paid for a profit of 113½ points.

Although it is possible that she could lose all of the premium cost, even that is not very likely. For that maximum loss to occur, the Disney stock would have to be exactly 130 at expiration of the options in December. In that case neither the put or the call would have any value and the total loss would occur.

But suppose Disney is at 135 when the expiration date arrives. Our client's 130 call would be worth 5 points and her loss would be reduced from 16½ to 11½ points.

Options traders anticipating wide price movements in a stock might employ long straddles.

Short Straddle

Markets are composed of differing opinions. While one client might expect Disney stock to have a wide price range in coming months, another might expect a quiet, uneventful period. This second client might consider using a *short straddle* and do the following.

Sell 1 Disney Dec 130 Call – Premium 10

Sell 1 Disney Dec 130 Put – Premium 6 1/2

He would receive 16½ points ($1,650) premium. If, as he anticipated, Disney did not rise above 146½ or fall below 113½ at expiration in December, he would retain some or all of the premium. For him to retain all the premium would be just as unlikely as it would be for the buyer of the straddle to lose the entire amount. For this to occur, the stock would have to be exactly at 130 at expiration. Possible but not probable. If Disney had declined to 126 in December, the put that he wrote would be worth 4 points, and he would retain only 12½ ($1,250) of premium.

While the client who purchased the Disney straddle had a maximum loss potential of $1,650 and an unlimited profit potential, the person who shorts the straddle assumes the opposite risk and reward. His maximum profit is the $1,650 of premium, and his maximum loss if the short call is uncovered is unlimited.

There are many variations of straddles but essentially they position the client on both the upside and the downside of the market. The long straddle requires wide price movement in either direction to be successful.

The short straddle will be profitable if the underlying stock experiences only minor price fluctuations prior to expiration.

A typical straddle uses the same number of puts and calls. In our example the client bought or sold short one Disney call and one Disney put. If the client felt strongly that the stock would be more likely to move in one direction than the other, he could adjust the number of options on each side.

STRIPS

A *strip* consists of two puts and one call on the same stock. If a client purchased:

1 Disney Dec 130 Call – Premium 10

2 Disney Dec 130 Puts – Premium 6½

his profit potential would be greatly enhanced if the stock declined in value. If Disney dropped to 110 at expiration, each of the 130 puts would have an intrinsic value of 20 points for a total of 40 points. His premium cost was 23 points (10 points for the call, 13 points for the two puts) so a 17-point profit would result.

If the stock rose, he would have to profit by 23 points on the one call, so a price of 153 (130 strike plus a 23-point premium) would be needed at expiration for the client to break-even.

STRAPS

A *strap* is a form of straddle that favors a rising market rather then a declining one. In a strap the client purchases two calls and only one put on the stock. If Disney stock rises to 155 at expiration, each of the calls is worth 25 points. This total of 50 points is offset by the 23 premium cost, leaving a profit of 27 points.

Strips and straps are forms of the straddle theory. They can be purchased or written (sold short). In these situations, the client simply has a stronger feeling about one market direction over the other.

COMBINATIONS

A straddle was defined as a put and a call on the same stock with the same strike price and the same expiration month. In a *combination*, the underlying stock is the same for both the put and the call, but the strike price and/or the expiration month is different. As with straddles, combinations can be long or short positions.

EXAMPLE: Long combination
    Buy 1 Disney Dec 135 Call – Premium 7
    Buy 1 Disney Dec 130 Put – Premium 6½

In this case the strike price for the call, 135, is different from the strike price on the put, 130. The premium for the call is less expensive than it would have been for a 130 call. The right to buy at 135 is not as valuable as the right to buy at 130. In our earlier example the 130 call commanded a premium of 10½ points. This 135 call was purchased for a 7-point premium. The buyer paid a total of 13½ points which he must recapture at expiration to break-even. When the December expiration arrives, Disney must be 13½ points above the call strike or

13½ points below the put strike for this to be achieved. Unlike a long straddle, this long combination leaves the possibility of a loss of the entire premium paid. If Disney is trading between 130 and 135 at expiration, neither the put or the call will have any intrinsic value and the entire 13½-point premium is lost. Figure 6.2 illustrates the potential for this combination.

EXAMPLE: Short Combination

Combinations, just as straddles, can be sold short as well as purchased. A client put on the following short combination:

Sell 1 Disney Dec 130 Call – Premium 10
Sell 1 Disney Jan 130 Put – Premium 9

Figure 6.2. Buy 1 Disney Dec 135 Call – Premium 7
Buy 1 Disney Dec 130 Put – Premium 6½

↑↓	Unlimited potential profit
Break-even (call) 148 1/2	
↑↓	Potential loss of 13 1/2 points
Call (strike) 135	
↑↓	Loss of entire 13 1/2-point Premium
Put (strike) 130	
↑↓	Potential loss of 13 1/2 points
Break-even (put) 116 1/2	
↑↓	Potential profit of 116 1/2 points

In this case, the strike prices are the same but the call expires in December, while the put does not expire until January. This additional month of time might raise the premium to 9 rather than 6½ had the put also expired in December.

The writer of the combination receives a 19-point premium and will retain all or part of it if the stock is not above or below the strike price of 130 by more than that amount at expiration. The writer has to wait an extra month for the put to expire, but for granting that additional time he received a large premium.

The risk and reward possibilities for the writer of a combination are just the reverse of those of a buyer of the same contracts. The writer's maximum profit is the premium received. His maximum loss may well be unlimited.

SPREADS

A *spread* is an option's strategy that is generally used only by professional traders. There are many varieties of this strategy, but the definition applies to all of them.

In a spread, the customer purchases one series in a class of options and simultaneously sells short another series in the same *class*.

Reviewing our earlier study, a *class of options* is all options of the same type (put or call) covering the same underlying security. A *series of options* is all options of the same class having both the same strike price and the same expiration month. Each class of options contains a number of series.

All IBM puts are a class. All IBM calls are a different class. In each class there are many series, the exact number depends on the number of available strike prices. As each strike price has three different expiration months, the number of series is determined by multiplying the number of strike prices by three.

Suppose the report of trading in options for XYZ stock

appeared as in Table 6.1. (All XYZ calls are a class. All XYZ puts are a class.)

Because there are four strike prices available, there are 12 series of options in each class. Each series has either a different strike price and/or a different expiration month.

The "spreader" will purchase one series in a class and sell (write) another series in that class. This simultaneous long and short position reduces the risk created if the spreader were just long or short. It also precludes the larger profit potential available if he were only long, or short rather than both. As options positions are measured, a spread is a conservative position. Nothing about options is truly conservative, but spreads are as close as we come.

All spreads create either a debit or a credit. If the option purchased had a higher premium than the one written, a debit would result. If the option sold produced a larger premium than the cost of the one purchased, the spread creates a credit. The *difference* between the two premiums is the *spread*. The goal of the investor is to have this spread either widen or narrow as the stock price fluctuates and the options approach expiration. In brief, the spreader hopes to make money on one side of the spread faster than he loses it on the other.

Spreads can use the same strike price but different expiration months. These are called time spreads or horizontal spreads. The horizontal nomenclature arises from the fact that

Table 6.1. Spreads

Options and NY Close	Strike Price	Calls—Last			Puts—Last		
		Nov	Dec	Jan	Nov	Dec	Jan
XYZ	50	7	8½	9½	⅛	¼	½
55	55	3	4	6	2¼	4	5
55	60	½	¾	1	6	7½	9
55	65	⅛	¼	½	12	13	14¼

the newspapers list the expiration months across the top of the page horizontally.

Spreads may use the same expiration month but different strike prices. These are called price or vertical spreads. The strike prices are listed vertically by the news media.

The spreads can be bullish, feeling the market will rise, or bearish, feeling that the market will decline. Let us look at a few of the possible applications of the spread strategy.

Time Call Spread Bullish

The XYZ 55 calls were priced as follows:

	Nov	Dec	Jan
XYZ 55	3	4	6
55			

If a client expected XYZ stock to attain higher prices, he might wish to purchase one of these calls. In the event of a price increase in XYZ the call expiring in January would be most likely to have the greatest increase in premium value. It has the longest time to run. The November and December expirations will be losing time value at a faster rate as their expirations near.

As a pure speculation, our client buys 1 XYZ Jan 55 call – premium 6. He spends $600 in the hope of making a profit, but suppose he is wrong and XYZ stock drops to $45 a share. His 55 call will have no value, and he would lose the $600.

The spreader takes a different approach. He would make this transaction:

Buy 1 XYZ Jan 55 Call – Premium 6

Write 1 XYZ Dec 55 Call – Premium 4

The $600 cost of the January call is partially offset by the $400 premium received for writing the December 55 call. He has established a spread with a $200 debit. If he is wrong and XYZ declines, he will lose only $200 not $600.

But if he is correct, he should show a profit. XYZ stock rises 3 points in value. The XYZ calls premium will also increase, but the longer calls will show a larger proportionate increase due to their additional time value.

Perhaps, after the 3-point rise, the XYZ 55 call premiums have the following values.

	Nov	Dec	Jan
XYZ 55	3	5	9
58			

With XYZ stock at 58, all of the 55 calls are 3 points in the money. As the November call is soon to expire, the premium may only reflect this in the money value. The December call may have an additional 2 points of time value as it has one month longer to go, for a premium of 5. But the January call may command a premium of 9, made up of 3 points intrinsic value and 6 points of time value.

Our client now closes out the spread by executing the following orders:

Sell 1 XYZ Jan 55 Call – Premium 9

Buy 1 XYZ Dec 55 Call – Premium 5

He shows a profit of 3 points on the January call which he purchased at 6.

He records a 1-point loss on the December call which he wrote at 4 and repurchased at 5.

Net Profit—2 points

Our client profited because the spread between the premiums widened. The original spread was 2 points—6 versus 4.

When he closed his position the spread was 4 points, 5 versus 9. The 2-point difference in the spread from the time he established it until he closed it became his profit.

When you establish a spread with a debit, you want that spread to widen. In our example it did, and the client made some money.

Time Call Spread Bearish

If a different client expected XYZ stock to decline, she might establish a bear spread by taking a position opposite of the bullish client.

She would:

Write 1 XYZ Jan 55 Call – Premium 6

Buy 1 XYZ Dec 55 Call – Premium 4

She has a credit of 2 points. She paid only $400 for the December call and received $600 for writing the January call. If she is correct and XYZ declines to $40 a share, both 55 calls will become worthless. The spread would have narrowed to 0. There would be no difference in the premium. She would keep the $200 credit. When a spread is established at a credit, you want that spread to narrow.

Here is a hint to remember the desired result of spreads:

Debit–Widen (each word has 5 letters)

Credit–Narrow (each word has 6 letters)

If our client had been wrong and XYZ had risen in price, she would have some protection. If the stock reached 60 she would be called on the January 55 she wrote, but she could exercise her December 55 call and purchase the stock at the same price. After her long call expires in December, however, she would be uncovered on the January 55 call, and the potential loss would be unlimited.

Price Put Spread Bullish

The XYZ Put premiums were priced as follows:

	Nov	Dec	Jan
XYZ 55	2¼	4	5
55 60	6	7½	9

Our first example of spreads utilized options with the same strike price but with different expiration months. Spreads can also be constructed using the same month but a different strike price.

An investor who is bullish on XYZ stock could put on the following spread.

Buy 1 XYZ Jan 55 Put – Premium 5

Write 1 XYZ Jan 60 Put - Premium 9

This investor established a credit of 4 points. He received a premium of 9 for the Jan 60 and paid only 4 to purchase the Jan 55.

If XYZ stock rises to 65, neither put will be exercised. At expiration in January they would be worthless. The spread would have narrowed from its original 4 points (9 versus 5) to 0 (0 versus 0). Our spreader keeps the $400 credit.

If XYZ declines to $50 a share our client will have some protection. The 60 put will be exercised against him, and he will purchase stock at $60 a share. He will then exercise his 55 put and sell stock for a loss of $500. This loss will be offset, however, by the $400 credit received on the spread, reducing the loss to $100. His maximum profit in the spread is $400, his maximum possible loss is $100.

Price Put Spread Bearish

A client who was bearish on XYZ stock would establish the opposite position:

Write 1 XYZ Jan 55 Put – Premium 5

Buy 1 XYZ Jan 60 Put – Premium 9

A debit of $400 would result, but if his market prediction was correct, he would share a profit. XYZ declines to $50 a share. The January 55 put will be exercised against him, but he will exercise the January 60 put. The $500 profit that would result is reduced by the original $400 debit leaving a profit of $100.

In the event that XYZ stock increases in value to $70, both puts would be worthless, and he would lose the $400 spent to establish the position.

He had established a debit spread. He wanted the spread to widen. In fact, however, it narrowed to 0, and he lost some money.

We have used only a small number of examples of spreads. The possible varieties are virtually endless, but the basic points in all spreads are the same:

1. Spreads may be established using either puts or calls.

2. Spreads may employ either different strike prices or different expiration months. (Sometimes both the strike and expiration month are different. These are called *diagonal spreads.)*

3. Spreads result in either a credit or a debit to the client.

4. Debit spreads are profitable if the spread widens, or if both options are exercised.

5. Credit spreads are profitable if the spread narrows, or if both options expire unexercised.

Let us look at the various forms of spreads using Table 6.2 which shows the market activity for XYZ options on a particular day.

Table 6.2. Market Activity

	Calls—Last			Puts—Last		
	Sep	Oct	Nov	Sep	Oct	Nov
XYZ 105	7	8	10	¼	½	1
112 110	3¼	4½	6½	½	1½	2
112 115	¼	2	4	2½	4¼	5½
112 120	¼	1	1½	8½	9½	11½

Note that XYZ's options expire in three different months—September, October, and November. Exercise prices have been established at four different levels—105, 100, 115, and 120. The previous day's closing market price for XYZ, $112 a share, appears under the name of the stock.

Table 6.3. Call Time Spread Bullish

	Calls—Last			Puts—Last		
	Sep	Oct	Nov	Sep	Oct	Nov
XYZ 105	7	8	10	¼	½	1
112 110	3¼	(4½)	(6½)	½	1½	2
112 115	¼	2	4	2½	4¼	5½
112 120	¼	1	1½	8½	9½	11½

Buy 1 XYZ Nov 110 Call @ 6½
Sell 1 XYZ Oct 110 Call @ 4½

This spread uses options that expire in different months so it is a time spread. Since the call purchased costs more (6½) than the call sold, the spread resulted in a 2-point debit. The client expects XYZ stock to rise. If this occurs, the premiums on the call options will also increase in value. But since the option that he purchased has one month more until it expires (November) than the one that he sold (October), that premium should rise to a greater amount.

If in mid-October, XYZ is trading at $115 a share, both options would have an intrinsic value of 5 points. Because the October option is near expiration, the premium is 5. The November 110 call may command a premium of 9 owing to its remaining month of life.

Our client could now close out his spread with the following orders:

Sell 1 XYZ Nov 110 Call @ 9

Buy 1 XYZ Oct 110 Call @ 5

His profit of 2½ points on the November call is partially offset by the ½ point loss in the October call. This leaves him a net gain of 2 points. The spread had widened from its original 2 points (4½ versus 6½) to its final level of 4 points (5 versus 9). The two points represents the client's profit.

Table 6.4. Call Time Spread Bearish

	Calls—Last			Puts—Last		
	Sep	Oct	Nov	Sep	Oct	Nov
XYZ 105	7	8	10	¼	½	1
112 110	3¼	4½	6½	½	1½	2
112 115	¼	(2)	(4)	2½	4¼	5½
112 120	¼	1	1½	8½	9½	11½

Buy 1 XYZ Oct 115 Call @ 2
Sell 1 XYZ Nov 115 Call @ 4

This spread again uses different expiration months with the same strike price. But this time the buyer is bearish. He expects XYZ stock to decline. By selling the November call at a premium of 4 and buying the October call at 2, he receives a credit of two points. If his thinking is correct and XYZ stock declines to $105, both the October and November options will become worthless. When they expire with no value, the spread will have narrowed to 0 and the client will retain the original 2-point credit as his profit.

Table 6.5. *Call Price Spread Bullish*

	Calls—Last			Puts—Last		
	Sep	Oct	Nov	Sep	Oct	Nov
XYZ 105	7	8	10	¼	½	1
112 110	3¼	4½	6½	½	1½	2
112 115	¼	2	4	2½	4¼	5½
112 120	¼	1	1½	8½	9½	11½

Buy 1 XYZ Nov 110 Call @ 6½

Sell 1 XYZ Nov 115 Call @ 4

These calls have the same expiration month, November, but have different strike prices. This is known as a price spread. Our client purchased the call with the low exercise price of $110 so the premium, 6½, was greater than the option sold, 4. The option sold had the higher strike price so the 2½ points difference is the client's debit. But, she is bullish. If XYZ stock rises to $120 a share, both options will be exercised. She will call at 110 and she will be called at 115 on the option she wrote. This results in a 5-point profit that is then reduced by the 2½-point debit that was incurred when putting on the spread. The client's net result is a 2½-point gain. It is important to remember that debit spreads are profitable if both options are exercised.

Table 6.6. Call ~~Time~~ PRICE Spread Bearish

	Calls—Last			Puts—Last		
	Sep	Oct	Nov	Sep	Oct	Nov
XYZ 105	7	8	10	¼	½	1
112 110	3¼	(4½)	6½	½	1½	2
112 115	¼	(2)	4	2½	4¼	5½
112 120	¼	1	1½	8½	9½	11½

Buy XYZ Oct 115 Call @ 2

Sell XYZ Oct 110 Call @ 4½

This above spread produced a 2½-point credit for the client. If his bearish view is correct and XYZ stock declines to $107 a share, neither the 110 call or the 115 call will be exercised. They will expire (and they will be worthless) and our client will keep the 2½-point credit as his profit. Credit spreads are profitable if both options expire unexercised.

Table 6.7. Put Time Spread Bullish

	Calls—Last			Puts—Last		
	Sep	Oct	Nov	Sep	Oct	Nov
XYZ 105	7	8	10	¼	½	1
112 110	3¼	4½	6½	½	1½	2
112 115	¼	2	4	2½	(4¼)	(5½)
112 120	¼	1	1½	8½	9½	11½

Buy 1 XYZ Oct 115 Put @ 4¼
Sell 1 XYZ Nov 115 Put @ 5½

A credit of 1¼ points has been generated by this put spread. Because the option purchased allows the holder to sell (put) the stock at 115 until October, it will naturally cost less than the option that allows the stock to be sold at 115 until November. Time has a value. It cannot be measured exactly but, in this example, the market tells us that the extra month is worth 1¼.

Remember that the client is bullish—he expects the stock to rise. If in fact it does go above $115 a share, neither put will be exercised. After all, who would want to sell (put) the stock at 115 if the market value was higher? In this scenario, our client would retain the credit of 1¼. If XYZ was trading at 125 neither put would have any value. The spread would have narrowed to zero and the client would make some money. Credit spreads are profitable if the spread narrows.

Table 6.8. Put Time Spread Bearish

	Calls—Last			Puts—Last		
	Sep	Oct	Nov	Sep	Oct	Nov
XYZ 105	7	8	10	¼	½	1
112 110	3¼	4½	6½	½	1½	2
112 115	¼	2	4	2½	4¼	5½
112 120	¼	1	1½	8½	(9½)	(11½)

Buy 1 XYZ Nov 120 Put @ 11½

Sell 1 XYZ Oct 120 Put @ 9½

Since the strike price of 120 is the same for both options, the 2-point difference is a function of the difference in time until expiration. The November put is worth more because its life is longer. In this case, the additional month is worth 2 points. The client is bearish so he has bought the longer and more expensive November put and sold the October. This has created a 2-point debit. As the expiration of the October put nears, XYZ stock is trading at $111 a share. The October 120 put has an intrinsic value of 9 points. However, because the October expiration date is near, the premium for this put may be only slightly above its intrinsic value, making it perhaps 10. The November 120 put also is in the money by 9 points, but owing to the additional month, the premium may be 13. The spread has widened from its original difference of 2 points (9½ versus 11½) to its current difference of 3 points (10 versus 13). When the client closes out the spread, he has a profit on the November put that he bought at 11½ and sold at 13 of 1½ points. When he repurchases the October option at 10, he loses ½ point since he originally sold it for a premium of 9½. Net profit equals 1 point. He had a debit spread. The spread widened. He profited.

Table 6.9. Put Price Spread Bullish

	Calls—Last			Puts—Last		
	Sep	*Oct*	*Nov*	*Sep*	*Oct*	*Nov*
XYZ 105	7	8	10	¼	½	1
112 110	3¼	4½	6½	½	1½	2
112 115	¼	2	4	2½	4¼	5½
112 120	¼	1	1½	8½	9½	11½

Buy 1 XYZ Oct 110 Put @ 1½

Sell 1 XYZ Oct 115 Put @ 4¼

In this situation, the put option our client sold gives the holder the right to sell (put) the stock at 115. This is obviously worth more than the client's option that allowed him to sell (put) at 110. Although the difference in strike price is 5 points, the spread between the option's premiums is 2¾ points. This 2¾-point credit is collected by our spreader. His market opinion turns out to be correct and XYZ goes up to $117 a share. Neither the October 115 put or the October 110 put will be exercised since the shares could be sold at a higher price in the open market. When the expiration date arrives in October, both options will expire worth nothing and our client will retain the 2¾-point credit as a reward for his astuteness. Credit spreads are profitable when both options expire unexercised.

But suppose our customer was wrong and XYZ stock had declined to $108. In this case, both options would be exercised. Our client would have to purchase 100 shares of XYZ at 115. He would then exercise his own put and sell at 110. This 5-point loss would be partially offset by the original 2¾-point credit, leaving him with a net loss of only 2¼ points. This is the true purpose of a spread. While it does limit the potential profit, it also lessens the possible loss.

Table 6.10. Put Price Spread Bearish

	Calls—Last			Puts—Last		
	Sep	Oct	Nov	Sep	Oct	Nov
XYZ 105	7	8	10	¼	½	1
112 110	3¼	4½	6½	½	1½	(2)
112 115	¼	2	4	2½	4¼	(5½)
112 120	¼	1	1½	8½	9½	11½

Buy 1 XYZ Nov 115 Put @ 5½

Sell 1 XYZ Nov 110 Put @ 2

When this spread is created, our client has a debit of 3½ points. But the difference in the strike price of the two puts is 5 points. If XYZ stock was to drop to $107 a share, the client would put the stock at 115. The put that he sold would also be exercised but under its terms the client would only be required to buy at 110. From this 5-point profit the original debit of 3½ points is subtracted and the resulting profit is 1½ points. If the stock behaves in a manner contrary to the client's belief and rises to 120, neither put will be exercised and his loss will be the original 3½ point debit.

DIAGONAL SPREADS

Up to this point our examples of spreads have been limited to time (horizontal) spreads and price (vertical) spreads. As we stated earlier, the terms horizontal and vertical are derived from the method used by the media in preparing the options tables. The expiration months (time) are arranged horizontally across the page. The strike prices are listed vertically. Time spreads use the same exercise price but different expiration months. Price spreads employ the same expiration month but employ different strike prices. Some spreads use both a different strike price and a different expiration month. These are called diagonal spreads. Let's look at one example of this trading strategy.

Table 6.11. Diagonal Call Spread Bullish

	Calls—Last			Puts—Last		
	Sep	Oct	Nov	Sep	Oct	Nov
XYZ 105	7	8	10	¼	½	1
112 110	3¼	4½	6½	½	1½	2
112 115	¼	2	4	2½	4¼	5½
112 120	¼	1	1½	8½	9½	11½

Buy 1 XYZ Nov 110 Call @ 6½

Sell 1 XYZ Oct 115 Call @ 2

Although this spread was created at a 4½-point debit, the option purchased has two decided advantages over the option written (sold). First, our client's call permits her to purchase XYZ stock at $110 a share while the option sold requires the holder to pay $115 a share. In addition, our client's call does not expire until November while the call that she wrote expires one month earlier. As our client predicted, XYZ stock was up to $116 by mid-October. The call that she sold with the 115 strike price would have an intrinsic value of 1 point and since expiration is near, the premium will not be much higher than that (perhaps it will be 1½). But the November 110 call that the client purchased is in the money by 6 points and still has more than one month before its expiration. This combination of values could command a premium of 12. If our client closes out her spread at these prices she would repurchase the October 115 call and show a profit of ½ point from the original sale price of 2. She would also sell the November 110 call at 12 for a 5½-point profit (since she had purchased it at a premium of 6½). The total profit, therefore, equals 6 points.

This spread widened from its original amount of 4½ (6½ versus 2) to its final difference of 10½. By subtracting the 4½ point debit paid in putting on the spread, we show a 6-point profit.

DISTINGUISHING SPREADS

Spreads can be created using a variety of elements, but three points are constant:

1. They employ either puts or calls

2. They are established at debits or credits

3. They are either bullish or bearish

Spreads can be either put or call, debit or credit, and bullish or bearish, so we should try to find an easy way to identify the distinguishing elements of each strategy. Perhaps the simplest method is to remember that each component of a spread contains a pair of opposites.

1. A put is the opposite of a call

2. A debit is the opposite of a credit

3. Bullish is the opposite of bearish

Perhaps Figure 6.4 will help you to distinguish the various elements of spreads.

Figure 6.4. Spreads Contain Opposites

	Put Spread	Call Spread
Bullish	Credit	Debit
Bearish	Debit	Credit

CHAPTER 7

Professional Uses of Equity Options

Equity options have become a valuable tool for professional investors and traders. They are often used to enable the professionals to reduce the risks involved in completing other transactions. A prime example of this would be in *block trading*.

A *block* of stock is an order to buy or sell a large number of shares of a security. While there is no precise definition of what minimum number of shares constitutes a block, it is generally considered that 10,000 shares or more would warrant this designation. But orders for many hundreds of thousands of shares are not uncommon in the securities industry. All major securities dealers have departments that seek out these orders from their institutional clients. The execution of these orders is a major source of revenue for the dealers.

Ideally, the brokerage firm hopes to represent both the buyer and the seller of the block, collecting a commission from each party to the transaction.

Suppose the block trading staff at Merrill Lynch receives an order to sell 400,000 shares of Ford Motors at $50 a share. The client is not interested in selling only a portion of the stock, he wants it sold "all or none." The Merrill people call other institutions that might have interest in purchasing Ford and find buyers for 300,000 shares. But that is not enough. Merrill still needs a buyer for the other 100,000 shares. To expedite the order, Merrill might purchase the remaining stock itself. It would charge the seller a commission on the sale of 300,000, and the buyers of that stock would also pay a fee. Merrill would buy the other 100,000 shares as principal, for its own account, and the transaction is done, with a nice profit for Merrill Lynch. But, there is a risk. Merrill owns 100,000 shares of Ford stock at a cost of $50 a share. If that stock drops to $45, Merrill might lose all of its profit and perhaps show a loss. In a situation such as this, equity options can come to the rescue.

Merrill might be able to execute the following order.

Sell (Write) 1,000 Ford Dec 50 Calls – Premium 3

Its long position has been protected by the 3-point premium received for writing the calls. If Merrill were forced to sell the 100,000 shares at 47, it would still be even. The 3-point loss in the stock is offset by the 3-point premium.

If Ford stock rose to 55, the calls would be executed against Merrill, but, as the calls are covered by the stock Merrill owns, no loss would occur. In fact, the gain on this transaction would be increased by $300,000, the 3-point premium Merrill received on each of the 1,000 calls written.

Naturally, there is risk. Should Ford stock fall below $47, Merrill will show a loss, but the use of the options has greatly reduced the risk and added a possibility of making an additional profit.

Instead of writing calls on Ford, Merrill could have purchased puts on the stock. In the event of a decline in price it could exercise the puts and sell the stock. But this would require it to pay a premium.

When given a choice of writing calls and receiving money, or purchasing puts and paying money, the options professionals will generally choose to write calls. They much prefer to receive than to give, and as professionals they are able to accept the financial risk. An individual investor might be more wise to pay for the protection by buying puts, as his risk would be limited. Professionals are in a different position.

Block traders can also use equity options to facilitate the execution of a large buy order. If a large client wanted to purchase 500,000 shares of Mobil Oil at 55, his brokers would search for sellers of that stock. If the search turned up only sell orders for 450,000 shares, Merrill might sell the remaining 50,000 shares short for the firm's own account. It might then protect the short position with options as follows:

Sell (Write) 500 Mobil Feb 55 Puts – Premium 4

If Mobil stock goes down to 51, the puts will be exercised, and Merrill will buy 50,000 shares at 55. But this simply covers the short sale that it made at the same price. No loss would result and Merrill adds the $200,000 premium received to its profit. If Mobil rises above 55, Merrill will be losing money on its short position. But with the protection of the 4-point premium, no overall loss would result unless Mobil went above $59 a share. There is risk involved, but the use of options has greatly reduced it while adding an additional possibility for enhanced profit.

Again, Merrill could have purchased calls on Mobil to protect against loss on the short position. But this would cost money which might be lost. It is better to write the puts and collect the money. The resulting risk is reduced, and the large order was executed. Risk is an everyday fact of life in the securities industry. Professional investors and traders are accustomed to accepting it.

RETAINING OPTIONS PREMIUMS

As we know, writing equity options earns a premium for the writer. Many professional investors have devised strategies that are designed to retain these premiums. By combining the options writing with other security positions, the risk of pure uncovered writing is reduced. In no case is the risk eliminated, but the reduction of risk together with the possibility of retaining premiums is accomplished.

While there are many such strategies, let us look at two of them, one is *bearish*, the other *bullish*.

1. Variable ratio writing

2. Long stock–short straddle

VARIABLE RATIO WRITING

This strategy would be used by a trader who felt a stock was due to decline. In order to study it completely let's review an earlier strategy—*covered writing*.

A client buys 100 shares of Exxon stock at $43 a share. She then writes the following option:

Write 1 Exxon Jul 45 Call – Premium 4

This call, of course, is covered, as she owns the 100 shares of Exxon and can deliver if exercised. She has protected her stock position by writing the call and receiving the premium.

Since she paid $43 a share for the stock, she could sell as low as $39 and still be even because the 4-point premium would offset the loss on the stock. If Exxon went up to 50, the call would be exercised and she would have to sell at the strike price of 45. Her actual sale price would be 49 when we include the 4-point premium received. Her profit would be 6 points.

Sale price   49 (strike price 45 plus premium 4)
Purchase price   43
              6 points profit

This is a relatively conservative position, as she has protected herself should the stock go down and will receive a reasonable profit should the stock rise. If the call is not exercised against her, she keeps the premium. She might then write another call and earn another premium.

In variable ratio writing a trader, feeling a stock is about to decline, would write more calls than he could cover. For example, he would buy 100 shares of Exxon at 43 and then:

Write 2 Exxon July 45 Calls – Premium 4

As he has only 100 shares of stock, one of the calls is covered, the other is uncovered. But he has received a total of $800 in premium, 4 points for writing each call. If Exxon stock went down as he anticipated to $41 a share, there would be little chance that the calls would be exercised against him. He could sell the 100 shares at 41 for a 2-point loss. But as he had taken in $800 of premium, his profit would be $600. This is called a 2-for-1 variable ratio write. He had only 100 shares but wrote two calls.

However, if our trader is wrong, and Exxon stock goes up, he faces the possibility of unlimited loss. He has written one uncovered call, and if it is exercised, he will be forced to purchase the stock in the market at whatever the price may be.

But this strategy has provided some protection. If exercised, he has to deliver 200 shares at $45 a share. He owns 100 shares and will show a profit of $200 on that stock as he paid only 43. In addition, he has an 8-point premium in his pocket which gives him some room if the stock goes up in value.

In this example, he could purchase the stock as high as $55 a share and still break-even.

The client is called on 200 shares of Exxon at 45. He delivers the 100 shares that he purchased at 43 and records a 2-point profit. He then purchases 100 shares of Exxon in the market at 55, resulting in a 10-point loss. But when we add the 8 points of premium to the 2-point profit we come out with a break-even position.

Purchase 100 shares @	55	Profit on 100 shares	$200
Deliver against call @	45	Premium received	$800
Loss	$1,000	Profit	$1,000

This protection is most helpful, but Exxon is above 55 when our trader is forced to purchase, he will show a loss.

The larger the ratio the greater the risk. If the trader purchased the 100 Exxon at 43 and wrote three Exxon July 45 calls premium 4 this would be a 3-for-1 variable ratio write. He would receive $1,200 in premium (4 points for each of the three calls written). If Exxon declined to 40, he could sell the stock purchased at 43 for a 3-point loss. But this would still leave him ahead by $900. He accomplished his goal. He took in a large amount of premium and managed to retain a good portion of it.

But if Exxon rises, he will be short 200 shares which must be purchased in the market. He has written three calls, and two of them are uncovered. To protect himself from loss, he has a total of $1,400. This consists of the 2-points profit of the 100 shares purchased at 43 and the $1,200 premium received.

But this must be used to protect him on 200 shares, meaning that he has only $700 of protection ($1,400/2) on each uncovered call.

As he must deliver at $45 if called, his break-even point would be 52 (45 strike plus 7 points for each call).

Buy 200 Exxon @			$52
Deliver against call @			<u>45</u>
	Loss		$700 per 100
	Total loss		$1,400
Profit on 100 shares			$200
Total premium received			<u>1,200</u>
	Total profit		$1,400

Ratio writing is a most risky strategy, and the greater the ratio the greater the risk. If the trader is wrong, he has a short position that must be covered. Being short even 100 shares carries unlimited risk. Being short 200, 300, or even more shares compounds this risk.

LONG STOCK–SHORT STRADDLE ✓

An options trader has an opinion that Warner Lambert stock will soon experience a major upward price move. He might look to profit by purchasing calls on the underlying stock. He might also write a put and retain the premium if the stock did as he expected.

But he could also employ a strategy that would increase the premium received and provide some protection if he turned out to be wrong. The following trade would be executed:

Buy 100 Shares Warner Lambert @ 110
Write 1 Warner Lambert Jan 110 Call – Premium 8
Write 1 Warner Lambert Jan 110 Put – Premium 7

He would now be long 100 shares of Warner Lambert stock and short a straddle on the stock expiring in January with a 110 strike price. He would also receive $1,500 of premium, $800 for the call and $700 for the put.

If his prediction were correct, and Warner Lambert stock goes up to $120 a share, the call he wrote would be exercised, and he would deliver 100 shares at 110. But the call was covered. He delivers the shares he purchased at 110, and no loss results. He profits by retaining the $1,500 premium. This is a far better result than would have occurred had he bought the call at 8 or written the put at 7.

But, as always, there is risk. Warner Lambert stock declines to 105. The short put will be exercised against him, and he must purchase 100 shares at 110. This makes him long 200 shares at that price—his original purchase and the exercised put. With the stock at 105, he has a loss of 5 points on each 100 shares, total $1,000. But he has $1,500 of premium, so he still has some profit remaining. The $1,500 protects him to the extent of $750 (7½ points) on each of the 100 shares. If the stock he purchased at 110 was sold at 102½, he would lose $1,500 in total and be even on these transactions. Any price below 102½ represents a loss. As he owns 200 shares, he will lose $200 for every point of decline below 102½. The risk is quite large but it has been reduced by the use of an options strategy. Had he purchased Warner Lambert stock at 110 his losses would begin as soon as the stock dropped below that price. Using a long stock—short straddle he has protected himself down to 102½ and may be rewarded by earning $1,500 of premium.

These are professional strategies and should not be used by the average individual investor. Many similar strategies exist, but our examples convey the philosophy.

The trader takes in a large number of premium dollars and hopes to keep all or most of them. If he is wrong he has some protection but losses can occur.

Professional investors may employ equity options to disguise their activities in a particular stock. A person or group may wish to acquire a large position in a security, perhaps 500,000 shares. To purchase this much stock in the open market may be difficult and may lead to a sizable increase in the value of the shares. In addition, purchases of such a large amount may become known to other investors who are able to analyze any increases in the trading volume of a particular issue. This may induce these investors to purchase that particular stock, making it more difficult as well as more expensive for the original buyer(s) to complete his program. As part of his strategy he may accumulate shares of the target company by purchasing call options.

For example, an investor desires to acquire a large block of Acme Can Corp. common stock currently trading at $27 a share. He wants to purchase the shares on the stock exchange without drawing attention to his activities. He places orders to purchase the stock in relatively modest amounts so that the orders go unnoticed by other professional traders. At the same time, he places orders to purchase Acme Can Corp. Jul 25 calls. Perhaps these calls have about one month until expiration and command a premium of 2¾. The total cost of the underlying shares to the investor would be 27¾ a share (stock price of 25 plus 2¾ point premium). While this is slightly higher than the market price of 27, there are certain advantages to this device. Purchase of the calls is not reported as part of the trading volume of Acme Can Corp. common stock and therefore is less likely to attract the attention of others. As the purchase of the options does not deplete the available supply of Acme shares, the investors may concurrently buy the stock more easily. In time, they might accumulate 2,000 calls which, when exercised, represent 200,000 shares of the underlying stock. If the investor's original goal was a total position of 500,000 shares, only 300,000 would have to be acquired in the open market. The use of call options may have minimized the risk of an acute price rise and may have allowed the investor to reach his goal without attracting attention that could have impeded his program. This strategy will not be effective in all situations; often it is not possible to purchase the desired options in sufficiently large numbers. However, it is a device that will often be helpful in achieving an investment objective.

While equity options can be used to implement programs, they cannot be used to circumvent securities laws or regulations. In an effort to provide the public with as much information as possible, the Securities Exchange Act of 1934 included regulations that require certain persons to disclose their activities in particular securities. These regulations are known as the insider requirements: An insider is defined as an officer, director, or principal stockholder of a company. A principal stockholder is deemed to be someone who owns or controls 10% or more of the company's outstanding stock. It is quite understandable that persons in these positions might be privy to information that is not available to the general public. If they took advantage of this inside information, it might cause damage to some other, less privileged stockholder. For example, a director of a corporation is aware that the company will report sharply increased earnings. As a result of this favorable development, the company will increase its dividend. When this information is publicly announced it will no doubt lead to a rise in the value of the shares. However, it has not been announced as yet so our "insider" purchases some of the shares. When the good news appears in the financial press he sells the shares at a profit and adds to his net worth. But we must remember that when he bought somebody else sold. Would this person have sold the stock had he known that good news was about to be announced? Probably not. Thus our director's profit came at the expense of a less fully informed investor.

If bad news was coming out, our insider might sell shares short and repurchase later at a lower price. Again the profit came at someone's expense. The director knew about the bad news, the buyer of his shares did not. In an attempt to equalize the position of all investors, the insider rules place certain requirements on those persons who may have important knowledge about a company's affairs.

There are four such requirements:

1. Insiders must report their holdings to the Securities Exchange Commission (SEC)

2. Insiders must report any change in their holding to the SEC

3. Insiders cannot sell stock short

4. Insiders cannot take profits in their stock within six months of purchase

With these requirements the noninsider will be informed of the activities of those with close contacts to the company. The public investor can use this information in determining his own market strategy. If, for example, he notices in the reports that many of the insiders are selling their shares, he might feel it is wise to do the same.

As time went on, the definition of an insider was extended to include any person who had access to nonpublic information. Thus investment bankers, accountants, attorneys, and many others are often bound by the same rules and subject to the same penalties as those directly associated with the company.

Equity options cannot be used to evade the insider rules.

Although options are not actually securities of the underlying company, they can be utilized in much the same manner.

Suppose the director who had advanced notice of the good news bought call options on the company stock instead of the stock itself. When the announcement was made, he sold the calls at a profit. As he had not actually traded in the stock has he successfully avoided the consequences? Not at all. While the call options are not actually shares of stock, they are what is known as equity equivalents. At the holder's option, they can be transformed into shares of stock and obtain all the benefits of stock ownership. Therefore, the insider requirement's apply to options just as they apply to the shares of the company itself. While equity options can be properly used to supplement a legitimate trading strategy, they cannot be a means of avoiding laws or regulations.

In the 1980s, market abuse led to the enactment of a rule regarding disclosure of ownership of a company's stock. During this period, market manipulators would acquire large positions in a particular target company. As the position was less than 10% of the outstanding shares, there was no need to report it to the SEC. Yet, in many companies, a position of less than 10% was sufficient to exert influence on the corporate management. The ownership of many companies is very broadly based. There are no single entities with extremely large holdings. Often management owns only a small portion of the stock. Thus if shares could quietly be acquired, even an 8% or 9% position in them could enable the shareholders to make demands. They might threaten to continue to purchase stock and take control of the company. If they were successful, they would discharge the current management and replace it with their own representatives. The current management, anxious to keep its position and lucrative pension plans, might therefore agree to buy back the shares from those threatening its future. Of course, the price to be paid would be well above the raider's cost but at least it would end the threat to the company. This practice became known as "greenmail"—the investment community's form of blackmail. Sometimes the raiders did not attempt greenmail but sought to take over a corporation in a hostile manner.

To prevent this form of manipulation SEC Rule 13D was enacted. This rule requires that a report be made if a person owns or controls 5% or more of a corporation's outstanding stock. Although 5% does not qualify the owner as an insider, a report similar in nature must be made. This report, in fact, goes even further. The party reporting under 13D must not only state his amount of ownership but must make known his future intentions. If he plans to increase that position perhaps to a point of control, he must make his intention public information.

Again, options cannot be used to avoid a rule. If a party owns stock and call options which in total represent 5% or more of the underlying stock a 13D report is required. No report would be necessary if options were purchased to acquire a position representing less than 5% of the stock. This might, in fact, be an intelligent strategy. But as calls are deemed to be equity equivalents for reporting purposes, ownership of them is tantamount to owning the underlying shares.

We demonstrated that an investor might use call options to assist in accumulating a large block of stock without attracting undue attention. Put options might serve the same purpose in facilitating the sale of a large stock position.

A client may desire to sell 300,000 shares of Best Oil Corp. The stock is currently trading at $34 a share but the stock trades in rather small volume. The sale of so large an amount might drive Best Oil down to $32 a share. Thus the client purchased Best Oil Feb 35 puts for a premium of 2. When he exercises the puts, he sells the stock at $35 a share. As the puts cost him 2 points, his actual sale price is $33 but this might be much better than selling in the open market.

Equity options are a very versatile product. They have many applications. Still, they can be of no assistance to someone who is seeking to avoid the rules.

Equity Options Accounts

Brokerage firms that handle options accounts exercise great care to protect both their clients and themselves from problems. As we have shown, the trading of options entails certain risks which are not present when dealing in other products. The client must be made aware of these risks so that she might determine if options are a suitable inclusion in her investment program. In addition to the obvious financial risks, there is a psychological risk. Options markets can be extremely volatile. A client accustomed to dealing in high-grade bonds and stocks may not be able mentally to handle the often roller coaster performance of options. The fact that options expire adds another dimension not present in other securities.

The brokerage firm must diligently search out information regarding the client to determine what type of options activity would be suitable for each client. It may be perfectly proper to approve a particular client's purchase of American Telephone stock or Con Edison bonds. It would often be totally improper to allow that same client to write uncovered puts and calls.

The broker wishes to avoid law suits and complaints from dissatisfied clients. To that end there are a minimum of three documents which are required when opening an options account for a customer.

1. Options disclosure statement

2. Options customer account agreement

3. Standard options agreement

OPTIONS DISCLOSURE STATEMENT

The options disclosure statement is properly titled "Characteristics and Risks of Standardized Options."

Space limitations do not permit us to reprint the entire document, but a copy of the cover and table of contents appear in Figure 8.1.

The complete document can be obtained from any securities dealer who handles options accounts. You will note that all options products are covered in detail. In addition to equity options, chapters are included which explain index options, debt options, and foreign currency options.

Most important, the risks inherent in the trading of options are fully explained. Other important items such as tax consideration, margin requirements, exercise, and settlement are included.

A new options customer must be provided with this booklet prior to or concurrent with the approval of that customer to deal in options.

Figure 8.1. Characteristics and Risks of Standardized Options

CHARACTERISTICS AND RISKS OF STANDARDIZED OPTIONS

Characteristics and Risks of Standardized Options

Stock Options

Index Options

Debt Options

Foreign Currency Options

TABLE OF CONTENTS

Having studied this material the client will be aware of the pitfalls that can be encountered in options trading.

OPTIONS CUSTOMER ACCOUNT AGREEMENT

All new accounts require a broker to prepare a new account record. When opening an options account, however, the firm will require more detailed information than is generally collected for nonoptions accounts.

The information is recorded by the registered representative who is handling the account. As you will note from the sample form in Figure 8.2, the necessary data goes far beyond the obvious items such as the client's name, address, occupation, and so on.

To properly determine the propriety of options trading for this person, the account agreement also shows.

Customer objective

Customer's approximate annual income

Customer's estimated net worth

Customer's previous investment experience

Type of trading desired

This document is signed by the registered representative and by the manager of the branch in which the account is being opened. The manager must have qualified as a registered options principal by passing the appropriate industry examination.

The customer account agreement must then be sent to the customer for her signature which verifies the information. The client must return the document to the firm within 15 days after approval of the account by the branch manager.

STANDARD OPTION AGREEMENT

The standard option agreement is also sent to the client for her signature and returned to the firm within 15 days of the approval of the account.

By signing this form, the client agrees to be bound by all rules and regulations governing the options market including

Figure 8.2. Customer Account Agreement for Equity and Index Options Trading

CUSTOMER ACCOUNT AGREEMENT FOR EQUITY AND INDEX OPTIONS TRADING

PLEASE PRINT: LAST NAME FIRST MIDDLE JMS OPTIONS ACCOUNT NUMBER & RR

HOME ADDRESS - STREET, APT. # | TELEPHONE NO.

HOME ADDRESS - CITY, STATE, ZIP CODE | CUSTOMER'S AGE | NO. OF DEPENDENTS | MARITAL STATUS

CUSTOMER'S EMPLOYER & OCCUPATION | BUSINESS TELEPHONE NO.

SPOUSE'S NAME (IF APPLICABLE)

SPOUSE'S EMPLOYER & OCCUPATION

CUSTOMER'S APPROXIMATE ANNUAL INCOME

☐ BELOW $15,000 • $15,000-$25,000 ☐ $25,000-$35,000 ☐ $35,000-$50,000 ☐ OVER $50,000

CUSTOMER INVESTMENT EXPERIENCE AND KNOWLEDGE

STOCKS ☐ ACTIVE ☐ AVERAGE ☐ NEW
BONDS ☐ ACTIVE ☐ AVERAGE ☐ NEW
OPTIONS ☐ ACTIVE ☐ AVERAGE ☐ NEW
ACCOUNT WITH JMS ☐ YES ☐ NO

SPOUSE'S APPROXIMATE INCOME (IF APPLICABLE)

COMBINED TOTAL INCOME FROM ALL SOURCES

TYPE OF OPTION TRADING DESIRED

☐ BUY CALL ☐ COVERED WRITING
☐ BUY PUTS ☐ UNCOVERED CALLS
☐ SPREADS ☐ UNCOVERED PUTS
☐ COMBINATIONS ☐ OTHER (SPECIFY) ______

CUSTOMER'S LIQUID ASSETS

CASH $ ______
SECURITIES $ ______
TOTAL LIQUID NET WORTH $ ______
OTHER ASSETS (Exclude Equity in House) $ ______
CUSTOMER'S TOTAL NET WORTH $ ______

OPTION ACCOUNT WITH ANOTHER FIRM (LIST BELOW)

FIRM NAME | FIRM NAME

ACCOUNT TYPE ☐ CASH ☐ MARGIN | ACCOUNT TYPE ☐ CASH ☐ MARGIN

Is this account to be operated by another person with power of attorney

☐ YES or ☐ NO

Name of person authorized ______

INVESTMENT OBJECTIVES:

SAFETY OF PRINCIPAL ______ INCOME ______

SPECULATION ______ OTHER ______

ACCOUNT APPROVED

______
REGISTERED REPRESENTATIVE

______
BRANCH MANAGER DATE

1. I understand that the trading of options is not suitable for everybody and I have been advised by representatives of Janney Montgomery Scott Inc. of the inherent financial risks of trading Options and I fully understand these risks. I further understand that the Option Market is a highly leveraged form of investment and as such contains a relatively high degree of risk.
2. I understand that the writing of uncovered or "naked" options is a highly speculative transaction which carries with it a correspondingly higher degree of financial risk.
3. I have received, read, and understand the option disclosure documents entitled "Understanding the Risks and Uses of Listed Options" and "Listed Options on Stock Indices" which were furnished to me prior to my initial option transaction.
4. The trading of options is in accord with my investment and trading objectives in light of my present and anticipated financial resources.
5. In the event my investment objectives, financial status, or type of option trading desired, should change, I will notify Janney Montgomery Scott Inc. promptly.

I understand Janney Montgomery Scott Inc., in accepting any orders for my account, will rely upon the information supplied by me and indicated on this form. I affirm that these representations are true and correct.

______
SIGNATURE OF CUSTOMER

______ DATE

______ SIGNATURE OF CUSTOMER (IF JOINT ACCOUNT)

Source: Used with permission, Janney Montgomery Scott Inc.

the position limits and exercise limits that were discussed earlier. Further, she agrees to permit the brokerage firm to use any money or securities held in her account to enable performance of any exercise made in her account.

The sample of a "Standard Agreement" found in Figure 8.3 is typical of those used throughout the industry. Careful study of all three of these documents is most important for all clients.

In turn, these papers enable the broker to determine what type of options activity, if any, will be permitted for each client.

DISCRETIONARY ACCOUNTS

A discretionary account is one in which the client permits the brokerage firm or one of its employees to enter orders for his account without first discussing the matter with the client.

Most often this authority is granted to the registered representative who handles the account. If the client has sufficient faith in the representative, he may permit him to enter orders to buy or sell options when it appears to be in the client's best interest. This saves time and might possibly prevent missing the opportunity to make a favorable transaction.

But there is obvious danger in granting discretion on one's account. The party holding this authority may apply it improperly or abuse the privilege by trading the account more frequently than necessary in order to create commission charges to the customer.

Brokerage firms, aware of these problems, place special conditions on the handling of discretionary accounts. Some firms in fact will not accept such accounts, but those that do require at least the following precautions.

1. All discretionary orders must be clearly marked as such.

2. All discretionary orders must be approved by the brokerage firm promptly.

3. All discretionary accounts must be reviewed by the firm at frequent intervals.

4. The discretionary authority must be granted in writing by the client.

Most individual clients would find no need to grant discretionary authority over their accounts. The representative handling their affairs should discuss each proposed transaction with them prior to executing orders on their behalf.

Figure 8.3. Standard Option Agreement

Janney Montgomery Scott
INC.

STANDARD OPTION AGREEMENT

Gentlemen:

In connection with any transactions executed by you on my behalf for the purchase and sale of put and call options I agree as follows:

1. All transactions shall be subject to the constitution, rules, regulations, customs and usages of the exchange or market and its clearing house, if any, where executed. If transactions are effected on a securities exchange, I further agree that I will not, either alone or in concert with others, violate the position or exercise limits which the Exchange may set from time to time.

2. (a) With respect to any call option which if exercised against me will require the delivery of securities sold, I will keep such securities in my account with you until the expiration of the option period, and will not sell or withdraw such securities. If the option is exercised you may deliver such securities to the purchaser without previous notice to me.

   (b) With respect to any put option which if exercised against me will require payment for securities purchased, I will keep in my account sufficient funds for such payment until the expiration of the option period, and will not withdraw such funds or utilize them for any purpose. If the option is exercised you may use such funs for the purchase of such securities without previous notice to me.

3. Any securities and funds held by you in any account of mine with you shall be held by you as security for the performance by me of my obligations to you under this agreement.

4. In case of my solvency, death or attachment of my property, you may, with respect to any pending options, take such steps as you consider necessary to protect yourself against loss.

5. This agreement is subject to the following arbitration clause, and in agreeing to abide by its terms, I acknowledge that:
   • Arbitration is final and binding on the parties to such a proceeding.
   • The parties to this agreement are waiving their right to seek remedies in court, including the right to jury trial.
   • Pre-arbitration discovery is generally more limited than and different from court proceedings.
   • The arbitrators' award is not required to include factual findings or legal reasoning and any party's right to appeal or to seek modification of rulings by the arbitrators is strictly limited.
   • The panel of arbitrators will typically include a minority of arbitrators who were or are affiliated with the securities industry.

   Any controversy between you and me arising out of your business, this Agreement or my account with you, shall be submitted to arbitration conducted under the provisions of the Constitution and Rules of the Board of Governors of the New York Stock Exchange, Inc. under the arbitration rules of any other national securities exchange of which you are a member or under the terms of the Code of Arbitration Procedure of the National Association of Securities Dealers, Inc., as I may elect. If I do not make such an election within five business days after receipt from you of a notice requesting the election, you may make the election on behalf of me.

6. Any agreement by me with you, whether previously or hereafter made applicable to any account of mine with you, shall also apply to such option transactions, except to the extent which it conflicts with this agreement. In the event of a conflict, this agreement shall control, and where there is no conflict, each provision of each agreement shall apply.

7. I understand that the writer of an option may be assigned an exercise notice at any time during the life of the option. I understand that exercise assignment notices for option contracts are allocated among customer short positions pursuant to a manual procedure which randomly selects from among all customer short option positions, including positions established on the day of assignment, those contracts which are subject to exercise. All short option positions are liable for assignment at any time. A more detailed description of the JMS random allocation procedure is available upon request.

8. THIS AGREEMENT CONTAINS A PRE-DISPUTE ARBITRATION CLAUSE IN SECTION 5. I ACKNOWLEDGE RECEIPT OF A COPY OF THIS AGREEMENT.

_____   _____
DATE   SIGNED

_____   _____
REGISTERED OPTIONS PRINCIPAL SIGNED
                             DATE

Janney Montgomery Scott
INC.
MEMBERS NEW YORK STOCK EXCHANGE INC.
AMERICAN STOCK EXCHANGE INC.   PHILA. STOCK EXCHANGE INC.

CUSTOMER COPY–PLEASE RETAIN

JMS114
FORM 5D (Rev. 8/89)

Source: Used with permission, Janney Montgomery Scott Inc.

More active traders, and those who use strategies that demand rapid decisions, may find that granting discretion is helpful.

The ultimate basis for the decision is the amount of faith you have in the person to whom you delegate this authority.

How many people would you trust with the key to your safe deposit box? Granting discretionary authority over your options account would be similar in many ways.

OPTIONS ORDERS

A detailed memorandum is prepared by a broker for each options order entered for a client. The order will record the time that the order was entered on the options exchange and the time at which the broker received the report of execution. In addition, the following items will be noted:

Client account number

Registered representative number

Exchange on which the option is traded

Method of receipt of the order

Buy or sell

Type of option (put or call)

Number of contracts

Underlying security

Expiration month

Strike price

Opening or closing transaction

Price limit or market order (best price available)

Type of account (cash or margin)

Was the order solicited or unsolicited?

Time duration of the order: Day—order is in effect only for this day. GTC—order is "good 'til canceled"

If order is for a straddle, combination, or spread

If account is discretionary

Client's name

Any other necessary instructions

Approval by the manager

Figure 8.4 is a hypothetical order for an equity option. While the order forms used by brokerage firms may vary to some degree, the information required is quite similar.

A record of these orders must be kept by the broker for a minimum period of three years after the order has been executed or canceled. This enables the client to verify all details should any question arise as to the handling of the transaction.

Upon execution of an options order, a *confirmation* of the transaction must be sent to the client promptly. While the registered representative will often report to the client by telephone, the written confirmation is required under the rules.

The confirmation will include the details of the transaction. Using our order example in Figure 8.4 the confirmation would show:

Underlying security: General Motors

Type of option: call

Expiration month: March

Exercise price: 45

Figure 8.4. Equity Options Order Form

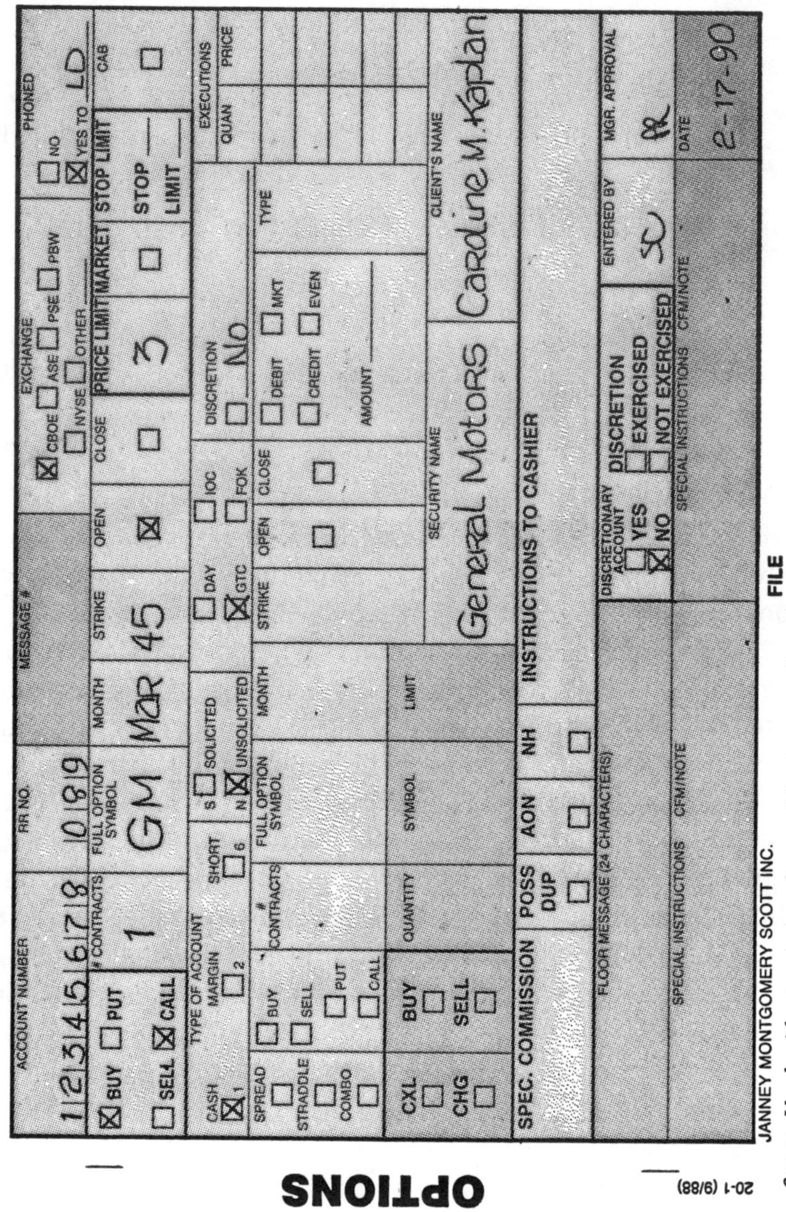

OPTIONS

ACCOUNT NUMBER 1|2|3|4|5|6|7|8 RR NO. 0|8|9 MESSAGE #

EXCHANGE ☒ CBOE ☐ ASE ☐ PSE ☐ PBW ☐ NYSE ☐ OTHER ____ PHONED ☐ NO ☒ YES TO LD

☒ BUY ☐ PUT ☐ SELL ☒ CALL # CONTRACTS 1 FULL OPTION SYMBOL GM MONTH Mar STRIKE 45 OPEN ☒ CLOSE ☐ PRICE LIMIT 3 MARKET ☐ STOP LIMIT STOP ___ LIMIT ___ CAB ☐

TYPE OF ACCOUNT CASH ☒ 1 MARGIN ☐ 2 SHORT ☐ 6 S ☐ SOLICITED N ☒ UNSOLICITED ☐ DAY ☒ GTC ☐ IOC ☐ FOK DISCRETION ☐ No EXECUTIONS QUAN PRICE

SPREAD ☐ STRADDLE ☐ COMBO ☐ ☐ BUY ☐ SELL ☐ PUT ☐ CALL # CONTRACTS FULL OPTION SYMBOL MONTH STRIKE OPEN ☐ CLOSE ☐ ☐ DEBIT ☐ MKT ☐ CREDIT ☐ EVEN AMOUNT ____ TYPE

CXL ☐ CHG ☐ BUY ☐ SELL ☐ QUANTITY SYMBOL LIMIT SECURITY NAME General Motors CLIENT'S NAME Caroline M. Kaplan

SPEC. COMMISSION POSS DUP ☐ AON ☐ NH ☐ INSTRUCTIONS TO CASHIER

FLOOR MESSAGE (24 CHARACTERS) DISCRETIONARY ACCOUNT ☐ YES ☒ NO DISCRETION ☐ EXERCISED ☐ NOT EXERCISED ENTERED BY SC MGR. APPROVAL

SPECIAL INSTRUCTIONS CFM/NOTE SPECIAL INSTRUCTIONS CFM/NOTE DATE 2-17-90

JANNEY MONTGOMERY SCOTT INC. FILE

20-1 (9/88)

Source: Used with permission, Janney Montgomery Scott Inc.

Number of contracts: 1

Premium: 3

Purchase or sale: Purchase

Trade date: February 17, 1990

Settlement date: February 18, 1990

Total amount due: premium plus commission

The confirmation will also disclose the capacity, principal, or agent, in which the broker acted on the transaction.

Principal would indicate that the firm sold the call to the client from the firm's own account. Agent indicates that it purchased the option from some other party and will charge a commission for its services.

STATEMENTS OF ACCOUNT

In addition to the confirmation of each transaction each client receives a statement from her broker periodically. This statement is sent each month if there was any activity in the account during that period. For accounts that are not active the statement must be sent each quarter.

The statement shows:

The market value of each option and security in the account

Total market value of all securities in the account

The margin equity (if a margin account)

The statement also advises the client to notify the broker of any material changes in the client's investment objectives or financial situation. This would enable the broker to revise the investment recommendations made to the customer.

A major concern in all aspects of investment is the suitability of a transaction to the particular customer. Even the most conservative securities, U.S. Treasury bonds entail some risk. Should prevailing interest rates increase, the market value of outstanding bonds will decline. A client forced to sell his Treasury securities because of some unforeseen emergency could well suffer a loss. The risk attached to bonds issued by corporations and municipalities will vary accounting to the financial condition of the issuer. Investors are assisted in their decision making by investment services that provide credit ratings for debt securities. The most notable of these services are Moodys and Standard & Poor's. The highest possible rating is triple A.

An investor requiring maximum safety for his portfolio might limit his purchases to bonds of this high quality. However, even this does not eliminate the risk of changing interest rates. If rates rise, bond prices fall. The risks entailed in buying stocks are as varied as snowflakes. Preferred stocks issued by high-grade corporations offer far less risk than the common stocks of new, unseasoned companies. Each investor must attempt to match his personal financial goals to the securities he selects for purchase. But even buying stocks of only the highest grade corporations does not eliminate market risk. The stock market is driven by emotional as well as financial factors. In some cases, the emotional factors outweigh the financial. When the market suffered the severe decline in October 1987, virtually all securities lost a large portion of their value. Many companies were experiencing record years of earnings but nonetheless the price of their shares declined. It was an emotional reaction not based on the factual condition of the individual corporation. When the market decline began to accelerate, investors took a "let's sell everything" attitude. Fear replaced logic and self-preservation became most people's goal. Better to sell now at a loss, they reasoned, than to chance a complete collapse and a total elimination of value. Naturally, as the selling pressure increased, the price decline became more severe. Those willing to buy stocks took advantage of the sellers' fear and made purchases at successively lower prices. Those who bought shares during these dark days were later proven to be correct, but it could have worked out differently. Fear is a natural protective shield. A healthy fear of a particular situation or condition can prove to be life-saving. But in markets it can lead to disruptions in the orderly process of investing.

Most investors can find bonds, preferred stocks, and common stocks that are suitable for their needs. This is not so with options. Most investors should avoid dealing in these products as the risks are beyond most of their abilities. While some strategies such as covered call writing are relatively conservative, they can lead to unfortunate results. The writer of a covered call may be compelled to sell his stock at a price far below the market value at the time of exercise.

For example, investor A writes:

1 XYZ JAN 50 Call – Premium 3

Because investor A owns 100 shares of XYZ common stock the call is covered. But suppose XYZ stock has a tremendous increase in value. The company introduces some revolutionary new product and the price rises to $90 a share. Investor A will certainly be exercised on the call that he wrote and will have to deliver the stock at $50 a share. When the 3-point premium received is added, his actual sale price is $53 but the stock is now at $90. By writing the call investor A did not increase his risk of loss but he certainly limited his potential for profit. This strategy is perfectly suitable for some, but not for all. Each investor must carefully weigh each decision.

The extremely speculative strategies, such as uncovered writing, should be left to professional traders. Taking risk is part of their vocation. It is an integral part of their earning a living. For example, firefighters are required to enter into burning buildings. Civilians should leave fire fighting to those trained in that skill. They should also leave uncovered options writing to the pros. The risk entailed in buying puts and calls is at all times limited to the premium paid to establish the position. As demonstrated, long option positions can effectively protect long or short positions in the underlying stocks. When utilized for this purpose both individual investors and professionals will find them beneficial. But long option positions can also be used to speculate. Again, in this application each investor must determine his ability to assume the risk of total loss of premium. If done within the strict confines of one's personal budget, it can cause little harm. However, if, as in many forms of speculation, it becomes an addiction, the danger cannot be measured. It is here that the investor's psychological condition is perhaps more a determinant than his financial status.

The brokerage firms that handle option accounts expend great effort to determine suitability. They are frequently subjected to law suits and arbitrations by disgruntled clients who lose money through trading options. In many cases, the client is justified. In many, he is not. There have been situations where the brokerage firm was clearly at fault. In one recent case, a charitable organization was induced to write uncovered calls. The representative of the firm who made this ridiculous recommendation was held to be liable. The firm that employed him was also found guilty for failing to properly supervise their employees' activities. Sometimes a client will bring a suit which is without merit but the brokerage firm must be prepared to defend itself. The documents that have been described in this chapter are most useful in building this defense. But suitability is not a concept that can be clearly defined. While two clients might have the same financial history, they might not have the same ability to assume the risk of options trading. Each situation must be judged independently. The brokerage firm attempts to do this for the good of the client as well as for its own protection.

However, no one knows you as well as you do. Therefore, you must make your own decision. No matter how many forms are filled out, or how many questions have been asked and answered, each investor is a case unto himself. By knowing what options are and how they can be used, your personal decision will be arrived at more easily.

Equity Options Margin

In this chapter two topics are addressed—the margin requirements for dealing in equity options and the tax consequences involved in equity options trading.

MARGINS

All credit restrictions in the United States are imposed by the Federal Reserve System (Fed). The regulation covering brokers extending credit on securities transactions is Regulation T. This rule states the minimum amount a customer must deposit (the margin) when purchasing securities or when sell-

ing securities short. The Fed imposes virtually the same requirements on banks that lend money on securities transactions under Regulation U.

In purchasing or selling short eligible stocks, the required
margin is 50%. Therefore, if you open an account at a brokerage firm and purchase 200 shares of IBM at a total cost of $110 a
share, your minimum deposit requirement would be $11,000.

Cost of purchase: $22,000 (200 shares at $110 a share)

50% margin: $11,000

The brokerage firm would lend you the balance of $11,000
and charge you interest on the loan. Your account would appear as follows:

Market value	$22,000
Debit balance	$11,000
Equity	$11,000

This is no different than buying a home. If the cost was
$100,000 you might put up only $20,000 and secure a mortgage
from a bank which would lend you the remaining $80,000.

Value of home	$100,000
Mortgage debit	80,000
Equity in home	$20,000

The Fed requirements for *margin on options* are quite different due to a fact that we have discussed before. Options expire.
They are wasting assets that at some time in the future become
worthless. Therefore, when you purchase equity options, you
are required to deposit 100% of the premium paid. The broker
cannot lend you any part of the purchase price, as to do so
would place him in jeopardy. If the options expire, and you

owe the broker money, he has no collateral for the loan. The broker might now be holding an account with a debit balance and no security. If the client cannot be found, the broker suffers a loss.

The 100% margin requirement for purchasing options is effective no matter what form of option is bought. If you purchase puts, calls, straddles, or combinations, you must deposit 100% of the premium cost.

EXAMPLE:

A client purchases:

10 LIN Broadcasting Feb 110 Calls – Premium 17

The margin required for this purchase is $17,000, 100% of the cost (10 calls at $1,700 each)

If at expiration in February LIN Broadcasting stock is trading below $110 a share, these calls would not be exercised. They would expire worthless. Had the broker lent the client any money to finance the original purchase, the firm would now have an unsecured loan on its books. Suppose the client left the country and gave no forwarding address—the broker would be the loser.

EXAMPLE:

A client purchases the following options:

1 Disney Jan 125 Put - Premium 7½

1 Disney Jan 125 Call - Premium 5½

As the underlying stock, the strike price, and the expiration month are the same on both the put and the call, this is a long straddle.

The required margin would be $1,300 comprised of the total premium for the put ($750) and the total premium for the call ($550).

This requirement again protects the broker against loss at expiration. If in January, at expiration, Disney stock was trading at $127 a share, the 125 put would have no intrinsic value, while the 125 call would have only $200 of intrinsic value.

Market price	127
Call strike price	<u>125</u>
Intrinsic value	2

If the broker had lent the customer 50% of the original cost as he could have done for the purchase of a common stock, his loss of $650 (50% of $1,300) would have been secured only by the $200 of intrinsic value.

EXAMPLE:
  The following options are purchased by a client:
  1 Tenneco Jun 60 Call – Premium 9
  1 Tenneco Jan 55 Put – Premium 5
  Margin required is $1,400, the total of the two premiums.

If at expiration Tenneco stock was at 57, both the 60 call and the 55 put would be worthless. Any loan made by the broker could possibly become a total loss.

MARGIN REQUIREMENTS FOR WRITING OPTIONS

As we have learned, the writer of an equity option is either covered or uncovered. If the writer is covered, no margin deposit is required. The stock or exchangeable product that he owns supplies the necessary protection for the broker.

If a client owns 100 shares of IBM stock and then writes:

1 IBM Oct 115 Call – Premium 6

no deposit would be necessary.

If IBM stock rose to $200 a share this call would certainly be exercised against the writer. But as the client owns the stock, he is in a position to deliver the shares. The same would be true if he owned a convertible security, a warrant, or a put on IBM stock.

As he is able to make delivery when called, no risk is present and no margin is required. In our example, in fact, the writer receives a premium of $600 for writing the option.

The same is not true of an uncovered writer. If the client wrote the IBM Oct 115 call uncovered, the risk involved would be unlimited. If the stock rose to $200 a share, he would be called at 115. As he is uncovered, he would have to purchase the stock at $200 to deliver at the strike price of 115. An 85-point loss would result.

Suppose the stock rose to $300 a share or $400, or $500, or $1,000?

As you can see, the potential loss cannot be measured. Therefore, a margin deposit is required under the rules of the Fed which provide protection for the broker who handles this position.

The requirement has been changed a number of times as market conditions have indicated the need. No doubt it will be changed again in the future, but at present the margin requirement to write an uncovered option is as follows:

20% of the Market value of the underlying stock

Plus the premium received

From this amount we subtract any out of the money amount.

Let's take this rule in two steps using the following example.

Write (uncovered) 1 IBM Oct 115 Call – Premium 6

Market Value of IBM 112

1. 20% of the market value of the stock plus the premium received
   Market value of IBM $11,200
   (100 shares at $112 a share)

$$\underline{X \quad 20\%}$$
$$\$2,240$$
Plus premium received $\underline{600}$
$$\$2,840$$

2. We must next determine if this option is in the money or out of the money. If it proves to be in the money we will do no more, and the margin required will be $2,840.

   If, however, it is out of the money, we will subtract that amount from the $2,840 to determine the requirement.

   Is this call in the money or out of the money?
   It is out of the money by 3 points.

The strike price of 115 allows the holder of the call to purchase 100 shares of stock at $115 a share. But the market price is only $112 a share. This option has no intrinsic value and is therefore out of the money.

To determine the margin needed we will subtract the out of the money amount.

20% of market value	$2,240
Plus premium received	600
	$2,840
Minus out of the money amount	300
Margin required	$2,540

Let's change this example slightly and make the option an IBM put rather than an IBM call.

Write (uncovered) 1 IBM Oct 115 Put – Premium 9½

Market Price of IBM 112.

1. 20% of the market value of the stock plus the premium received
   Market value of IBM $11,200
   (100 shares at $112 a share)

$$\underline{X \quad 20\%}$$
$$\$2,240$$
Plus premium received $\underline{950}$
$$\$3,190$$

2. If this put is out of the money, we would now subtract the out of the money amount. But the option is in the money. It gives the holder the right to sell (put) 100 shares of IBM stock at $115 a share. The market price of the stock is $112 a share giving this put option an intrinsic value of $300.

   As the put is in the money, we make no further adjustment.

Margin required – $3,190

These requirements are computed each day. If they increase, the client will be notified to deposit any additional amount promptly. If he fails to do so, the broker will liquidate the position to prevent any loss.

For example, suppose IBM stock declines to $108 a share, and the premium on the put increases to 14 ($1,400).

Let's recompute the margin.

Market value of IBM $10,800
($108 a share)

$$\underline{X \quad 20\%}$$
$2,160
Plus current premium   1,400
$3,560

The required margin has increased to $3,560. Had the client deposited the original amount of $3,190, he would now be notified to deposit an additional $370 immediately.

Current margin requirement $3,560
Original requirement   3,190
Additional deposit $ 370

In periods of wide market fluctuations, the writer of an uncovered put or call may be required to deposit additional margin regularly to maintain his position. This adds to the risks of this type of options activity.

MINIMUM MARGIN REQUIREMENTS

If a client were to write an uncovered equity option that was deep out of the money, the required margin, using the usual method of determination, might be quite small. In some cases we would even arrive at a negative figure.

For example, if a client wrote the following put uncovered:

1 XYZ Aug 25 Put - Premium ¼

Market price of XYZ - 30

Using the regular method of calculating margin

Market value	$3,000
	X 20%
	600
Plus premium	25
	625
Minus out of the money	500
Margin required	$125

The put has a strike price of 25. As the stock is trading at 30, the option is 5 points out of the money. When we subtract this amount, we are left with only a $125 margin requirement. This does not provide much protection for the broker.

There are times, in fact, when the subtraction of the out of the money amount leaves us with a negative requirement.

EXAMPLE:

Write (uncovered) 1 ABC Jul 30 Call – Premium ½

Market Price of ABC 24

Let's compute margin using the usual system:

Market price of ABC	$2,400
	20%
	$480
Plus premium	50
	$530
Minus out of the money	600
Margin required	-$70

As a negative requirement has resulted, the client would not have to make any deposit. The broker would be in trouble if the market rose rapidly which is certainly possible.

To reduce the possibility of loss to the firm handling the account, there is a minimum margin required for writing any uncovered equity option.

The minimum requirement would be:

10% of the market price of the stock
plus the premium received

We will look at our two previous examples using this minimum requirement

Write (uncovered) 1 XYZ Aug 25 Put – Premium ¼

Market price of XYZ – $30

Market price of XYZ	$3,000
	X 10%
	$300
Plus premium	25
Minimum requirement	$325

When we used the standard method of computation, we arrived at a requirement of $125. As the minimum requirement of $325 is greater, it is that amount that would apply.

The same is true in our other example:

Write (uncovered) 1 ABC July 30 Call – Premium ½

Market Price of ABC – 24

The minimum requirement would be:

Market price of ABC	$2,400
	X 10%
	$240
Plus premium	50
	$290

This $290 figure is certainly greater than the -$70 which was the result of the usual calculation.

Again, in this case the minimum requirement would be the margin necessary for this position.

Note that this minimum will only apply if the option writen is *deep* out of the money. The subtraction of this amount greatly reduces the required deposit and could endanger the broker.

The requirements we have demonstrated have been established by the Fed. Individual brokerage firms can, and often do, set higher requirements to add to their protection.

Each client should be aware of the rules of the firm with which he transacts his business.

STRADDLES AND COMBINATIONS

As we have seen, a *straddle* or *combination* consists of a put and a call on the same underlying security. In a straddle, both the strike price and the expiration month are the same. In a combination, either the strike price and/or the expiration month is different. In determining the amount of margin required for these positions, we use the same procedure. If the client puts on a long straddle or long combination, he must pay both premiums in full. Long options have no loan value. The client pays in full.

EXAMPLE:

> Buy 1 XYZ JUN 50 Call – Premium 3
> Buy 1 XYZ JUN 50 Put – Premium 2½

The margin required for this long straddle is $550. This consists of the premium for the long call ($300) plus the premium for the long put ($250).

The margin required for a short straddle or short combination is computed by separately figuring the requirement for both the put and the call. The larger of the two amounts is then taken and the premium from the other position is then added.

EXAMPLE:

> Uncovered Short Straddle
> Sell 1 XYZ SEP 70 Put – Premium 6
> Sell 1 XYZ SEP 70 Call – Premium 2
> Current Market Price of XYZ – 68

Put computation:

20% of market value ($6,000)	$1,360
Plus premium	$ 600
Total	$1,960

(Note: As this put is in the money, no further adjustment is made.)
Call computation:

20% of market value ($6,800)	$1,360
Plus premium	$ 200
	$1,560
Minus out of the money amount	$ 200
Total	$1,360

The requirement for the put, $1,960, is greater than that for the call, $1,360. To the put requirement, the premium for the call ($200) is added and the total requirement of $2,160 ($1,960 put requirement plus $200 call premium) is concluded.

The complete process used in this computation has now been demonstrated but usually it would not be necessary for this type of position. In the case of a short straddle, in most every situation, one side is in the money and the other is out of the money. The in the money side will always have the greater requirement as the premium will be greater and there is no subtraction for any out of the money amount. It is, therefore, usually only necessary to compute the in the money side and add the premium from the other option.

UNCOVERED SHORT COMBINATION
Sell 1 XYZ OCT 50 Put – Premium 1½
Sell 1 XYZ NOV 50 Call – Premium 5½
Current Market Price of XYZ – 53
Put calculation:

20% of market value ($5,300)	$1,060
Plus premium	$ 150
	$1,210
Minus out of the money amount	$300
Total	$ 910

Call calculation:

20% of market value ($5,300)	$1,060
Plus premium	$ 550
Total	$1,610

As expected, the in the money side (call) had a greater requirement than the out of the money side (put). To this call requirement of $1,610, the premium for the put, $150, is added for a total amount of $1,760.

UNCOVERED SHORT COMBINATION
    Sell 1 XYZ JAN 90 Put – Premium 7
    Sell 1 XYZ JAN 85 Call – Premium 3
    Current market price of XYZ – 86

    In this example, the expiration month is the same for both the put and the call but the exercise prices are different. In fact, a situation has been created in which both sides are in the money. As the market price of XYZ is 86, the put with the 90 strike price is 4 points in the money; and the call with a strike price of 85 is 1 point in the money. In this type of situation, only the option with the largest premium has to be calculated. As the 20% of the market value is the same for both options, the only difference is the premium to be added. Both calculations will be demonstrated but only one would be necessary.

Put calculation:

20% of market value ($8,600)	$1,720
Plus premium	$ 700
Total	$2,420

Call calculation:

20% of market value ($8,600)	$1,720
Plus premium	$ 300
Total	$2,020

    To the $2,420 requirement for the put, the $300 premium is added in the call for a total of $2,720.

As always, the calculation is reviewed each day and any increase in the amount of margin required will be deposited by the client.

SPREADS

Spread positions can be created using either puts or calls. In either case, the client buys one option on a particular security and writes (sells) a different option covering that same security. The main consideration in determining the margin on a spread is whether the position is covered or uncovered. A covered position is one in which the long option has an expiration no earlier than the one sold short and that the strike price on the long option is at least as favorable as the option sold.

EXAMPLE:
   Buy 1 XYZ MAR 55 Call – Premium 7
   Sell 1 XYZ MAR 60 Call – Premium 3

As both options expire in March, there is no time difference. In addition, the call purchased has a lower strike price (55) than the option written (60). If XYZ stock was up to $100 a share, both options would be exercised. Our client would have to deliver stock at $60 a share but he would purchase the shares at $55 by exercising his long call. The position presents no danger to the broker handling the account, therefore, no margin would be required for the spread. The customer would have to deposit the difference in premiums paid and received. As his long call cost $700 and he was paid only $300 for the call written, he would be required to deposit $400.

However, if the spread is uncovered, the broker will be in danger and the margin will be necessary to provide him with protection.

There are two ways in which a spread can be uncovered. First, if the strike price of the long option is less favorable than that of the option sold short. And, second if the long option expired sooner than the option written.

Example:

Buy 1 XYZ FEB 55 Put – Premium 2

Sell 1 XYZ FEB 60 Put – Premium 5½

As both options expire in February, no time problem exists. But the strike price on the long put (55) is less favorable than on the option written (60). If XYZ stock drops to $30 a share, our client will be put and have to pay $60 a share for XYZ stock. As his long option allows him to sell at $55, a 5-point loss ($500) will result. But $500 is the maximum danger to the broker. Therefore, the margin required in this situation will be the difference in strike prices. As paid 2 ($200) for the long position and received 5½ ($550) for writing $500, this $350 can be applied against the $500 due.

EXAMPLE:
    Buy 1 XYZ OCT 60 Call – Premium 3
    Sell 1 XYZ DEC 60 Call – Premium 8
    Current Market Price of XYZ – 62

Here we have a difference that cannot be measured in dollars. The strike prices are identical but the long option expires two months sooner than the one sold short. In the previous example, it was a simple matter to measure the difference in value of different strike prices. But, how can a dollar value be placed on two months of time? It cannot. Once the October options expire, the client position simply becomes that of an uncovered call writer.

As seen, an uncovered call position carries unlimited risk. Therefore, this position is treated as any uncovered call would be treated and the client would be required to deposit the normal margin. He must also put up the premium paid for the option that he purchased.

Calculation

Short Call

20% of market value ($6,200)	$1,240
Plus premium	$ 800
Total	$2,040
Long call premium (3)	$ 300
Total margin required	$2,340

In a sense, the options margin requirements are designed to protect the broker. If there is no danger, such as writing a covered call, there is no margin. If the danger is measurable as in long options positions or some uncovered spreads, the client must deposit the amount for which the broker would be at risk. If the danger cannot be measured in dollars, uncovered calls for example, then the normal margin requirements will be in effect.

TAXES ON OPTIONS

Tax considerations are an important factor in investment planning. Each individual's situation varies, and no blanket approach can be effective. It is not the purpose of this book to give tax advice. That can only be done by a competently trained accountant who is familiar with a client's total financial situation. We can, however, outline the fundamental tax factors that are concerned with the trading of equity options.

BUYING AND SELLING OPTIONS

If a person buys and sells an equity option, the result for tax purposes is as if she had bought and sold a stock. When the position is closed out, she will have either a capital gain or a capital loss. Consider the following transactions.

Feb 20, 1990, Buy 1 Dow Jun 90 Call - Premium 5

May 20, 1990, Sell 1 Dow Jun 90 Call - Premium 7½

The result is a $250 (2½ point) capital gain for the client. This gain is added to gains from other capital transactions for tax purposes. The total of gains is then offset by any capital losses to determine tax liability.

As we have seen, an options client often begins her position by writing an option and later closes out by repurchasing the contract.

Aug 10, 1990, Write 1 CBS Sep 210 Put - Premium 5

Sept. 8, 1990, Buy 1 CBS Sep 210 Put - Premium 8

These trades resulted in a $300 (3 point) loss to the client. She sold the put at a premium of 5 and repurchased for a premium of 8. This loss becomes one element in determining her tax situation for that year.

At times the tax law applies different treatment to long- and short-term gains and losses. If this is the case at the time options transactions are made, it is the length of time that the client held the option that will determine into which category it falls.

OPTIONS EXPIRATION

The unique feature of options is that they expire. If you own IBM stock you might hold your position for many years.

This is not true if you own an IBM option. At a given future date that option expires and becomes worthless.

To study the tax situation at the expiration of an option we must consider the two possibilities that will exist at that time.

1. The option will be worthless and will expire unexercised.

2. The option will have an intrinsic value and will be exercised.

We will look at these possibilities separately.

Unexercised Options

Client Jones purchases, and client Smith writes the following equity option

1 Motorola Dec 60 Call - Premium 3

At expiration in December, Motorola stock is at $57 a share. This call with a strike price of 60 has no intrinsic value and will expire unexercised.

How do we treat the $300 premium from a tax standpoint?

When an option expires unexercised, the premium becomes a capital loss to the purchaser and a capital gain to the writer.

It is treated as though a trade took place at expiration at a price of 0.

The Motorola Dec 60 call that Jones purchased at 3, he, in effect, sells at 0. The result is a $300 loss.

The Motorola Dec 60 call that Smith sold (wrote) at 3, she repurchases at 0. The result is a $300 gain.

In actuality, no such transaction occurred, but for tax purposes it is as though one did take place.

Exercised Options

When an option is exercised, it is considered to be a transaction in the underlying stock. In the case of a call, the holder of the option purchases the stock while the writer of the options sells the shares.

The opposite occurs when a put is exercised. The holder of the put sells the stock, while the put writer purchases it. To determine the price at which this trade takes place, we must consider two factors, the strike price and the premiums.

When a call is exercised, we add the premium to the strike price to determine the price at which the stock changed hands.

When a put is exercised, we subtract the premium from the strike price to determine the price of the transaction.

EXAMPLE: EXERCISED CALL

June 10, 1990, Client Smith purchases, and client Jones writes the following option:

1 Abbott Aug 65 Call - Premium 3½

On August 17, 1990, just prior to expiration, Abbott Labs is trading at $70 a share, and Smith exercises his call against Jones.

On that date, August 17, 1990, Smith purchases and Jones sells 100 shares of Abbott Labs at 68½ a share.

Strike price	$65
Plus premium	3½
Transaction price	$68½

At time of exercise, Smith pays the $65 strike price, but he had also paid 3½ points for the call. His true cost is 68½, the total of these two elements.

Jones receives $65 a share upon exercise but she also received a 3½-point premium when she wrote the call. Her total proceeds amount to 68½ a share. To determine the tax effect we would need further information.

Suppose Smith immediately sells the stock in the market at $70. He would have a $150 (1½ point) capital gain. He purchased at 68½ and sold at 70.

But perhaps he holds the stock for five years and then sells it at $100 a share. A capital gain of $3,150 would result. The stock was purchased for $6,850 (68½) and sold for $10,000 (100). Had Smith sold the stock for less than 68½, he would record a capital loss on the transaction.

In simple terms, Smith has purchased 100 shares of Abbott Labs at 68½ on August 17, 1990. When he later sells it, we compare the sale price to this cost to determine his gain or loss.

How about client Jones, the writer of the call?

She has sold 100 shares of Abbott Labs at 68½ on August 17, 1990. To determine her tax liability, we again need more information.

Suppose she delivers Abbott stock purchased many years earlier at $40 a share. She shows a capital gain of $2,850 (28½) points).

Sale price 68½:	$6,850
Cost 40:	4,000
Gain	$2,850

However, suppose Jones had written the call uncovered. When it was exercised she would have been forced to go into the market and buy the stock at $70 a share. When measured against her sale price of 68½, her loss for tax purposes is $150.

EXAMPLE: EXERCISED PUT

Oct 14, 1990, Client Smith purchases and client Jones writes the following option.

1 GM Dec 55 Put - Premium 4½

On December 15, 1990, just prior to the expiration of the

put, General Motors stock is trading at $48 a share and Smith exercises his put against Jones.

On that date Smith has sold (put), and Jones has bought 100 shares of General Motors at $50½ a share.

Strike price	$55
Minus premium	4½
Transaction price	$50½

When Smith exercised his put, he received the strike price of $55 a share. But he had paid 4½ points ($450) to purchase the option, leaving him with net proceeds of $5,050 (50½).

His tax situation will be determined by comparing this sale price against his cost for the stock. If he delivered shares purchased at $30, his gain would be $2,050.

Sale price	50½:	$5,050
Cost	30:	3,000
Gain		$2,050

If he delivered shares purchased at $60 a share his loss would be $950.

Cost	60:	-$6,000
Sale price	50½:	-5,050
Loss		$950

The writer of the put, Jones, has purchased stock at 50½. That is her cost, and her tax situation will be determined when she sells the shares.

Suppose Jones is a patient investor and holds the shares for three years. She is rewarded as the price rises to $70 a share at which point she sells. Profit $1,950.

Sale price	70:	-$7,000
Cost	50½:	5,050
	Gain	$1,950

The exercise of an equity option simply determines the price of a transaction.

Call—strike plus premium = transaction price

Put—strike minus premium = transaction price

In each case, one party has bought stock, and the other party has sold it. The tax situation can easily be determined when we add one more factor.

At what price did the buyer sell the stock?

At what price did the seller buy the stock?

The answer to these questions enables us to compute the client's capital gain or capital loss.

CHAPTER 10

Other Options Products

While we have concentrated our study on options on equity securities, it is important to include a brief discussion of options issued on other underlying products.

Options are traded on three other business related items:

1. Stock indexes

2. Foreign currencies

3. Debt securities (interest rate options)

The principles used in trading these options is the same as with equity options. A put is still a put, a call is still a call. But the applications of these other contracts provide different methods of speculating on or protecting against future events.

While we will make no attempt to cover all aspects of these contracts an introductory study will add to our overall options knowledge.

INDEX OPTIONS

A stock index is a method of depicting the changing market values of a large number of securities in a single number. The most often quoted stock index is the Dow Jones Industrial Average. This index consists of the weighted average of 30 actively traded stocks of industrial corporations. When a newscaster reports that the market "was up 5 points today" he is usually referring to a 5-point increase in the Dow Jones Industrial Average. Despite the comparatively small number of components, the "Dow" has been the major instrument used to measure market movements.

There are numerous other market indexes which contain far more components. Some are designed to measure overall market changes while others confine their reading to a particular industry such as computer stocks, transportation companies, or utility shares.

An investor is not able to purchase an index. It is used as a measuring device. A person could purchase all of the stocks used in the index, but that would be a most expensive proposition. Imagine buying all of the stocks that are included in the Standard & Poor's 500 stock index. Such an expenditure would be beyond the ability of all but the largest institutional investors.

There has developed, however, a method of making actual investments based on the projected movement of these market indicators. It is called an index option.

Just as one can purchase or write a put or a call on General

Electric stock, one can also apply the same techniques to trade stock indexes. Three of the major indexes on which options may be traded are:

Standard & Poor's 100 Stock Index

Standard & Poor's 500 Stock Index

Major Market Index

Standard & Poor's (S&P) 100 Stock Index options is traded on the CBOE, the S&P 500 Stock Index is traded on the CME, and the Major Market Index options trade on the American Stock Exchange. As is the case with equity options, all index options are issued and cleared by the OCC.

A major distinction between equity options and index options is the method of settling upon exercise.

If you owned a Delta Airlines Nov 65 call, and you exercised your option, the writer who was exercised against would deliver 100 shares of Delta stock at $65 a share.

This would not be possible with index options. If you owned a call on the S&P 100 Stock Index and exercised the option you certainly would not expect the writer to deliver 100 shares of 100 different stocks.

No, index options are settled in cash. Let's use the S&P 100 Index option as our example. Although other index options are traded daily, this particular option is generally the most active.

Each day a closing price is set for the index, just as each stock traded on the exchanges has a closing price. Suppose on a given day the closing price for the S&P 100 Index was 320.00. A multiplier, usually 100, is used to determine the dollar value of the index. In this case the value would be $32,000 (320.00 times 100).

If you owned an S&P 100 call with a strike price of 315.00, the exercise value of the option would be $31,500 (315.00 times

100). If you exercised the call, the writer would deliver to you the cash difference between your strike price and the actual value. You would receive $500 in cash.

If you had paid a premium of 2 ($200) to purchase the call, your net profit would be $300 ($500 cash less $200 premiums).

With the S&P Index set at 320.00, a client exercises an S&P put with a strike price of 330.00. The writer of the put will pay her $1,000. This is the difference between her sale (put) price of $33,000 (330.00 times 100) and the actual value of $32,000 (320.00 times 100).

So the outcome is quite similar to the trading of equity options. Just the method of settlement varies. On the exercise of an equity option, shares of stock change hands. When an index option is exercised, money is delivered by the writer.

Index options can be used to accomplish many of the same results as equity options and in some ways can accomplish more.

Suppose you thought that IBM stock was going to go higher in price. You buy an IBM call. But much to your dismay, every stock on the exchange goes up except IBM. While others are celebrating a rising market, you are counting your losses.

If, however, you had bought a call on the S&P 100 Stock Index, it would not be necessary for all 100 stocks to rise in order for you to profit. If the market in general rose, the value of the index would most probably rise, and you would be wearing a smile.

Most of the aspects of trading index options are the same as with stock options. The strike prices and expiration months are established by the exchange on which the options trade. The buyer and sellers are left only the premium to negotiate.

If you though the market in general would rise, you might use index options just as we used stock options.

Up | buy (long) calls
side | write (short) puts

If you saw the general market lower in the near future, you would take the opposite approach.

Down ⎤ buy (long) puts

side ⎦ write (short) calls

As Figure 10.1 shows, index options are quite actively traded. On the date in question, all 10 of the most active options on the CBOE were S&P 100 Stock Index options and three of the American Stock Exchange's 10 most active options were based on the Major Market Index.

PROFESSIONAL USES OF INDEX OPTIONS

While individual investors can use index options to protect positions or to speculate as they do with equity options, the product finds its greatest application with professional investors.

Index options permit managers of large pools of money to protect their positions and to participate in the market with a minimal amount of dollar cost.

Let's assume the manager of the Toxic Waste Manufacturing Company's pension fund has a portfolio of $100 million worth of stocks to look after. His investment analysis tells him that the stock market is about to suffer a decline that will cause major shrinkage in the value of the portfolio.

What can he do?

To sell all the stocks in the portfolio might be impractical if not impossible. To provide the money needed to pay employee pensions, the funds must be invested. When the decline is over he will be forced to make new investments that might not prove to be as attractive. In addition, to dispose of a portfolio of this size might necessitate forcing down the price of the securities· because of the weight of his selling program.

Figure 10.1. Most Active Options

MOST ACTIVE OPTIONS

CHICAGO BOARD

CALLS

		Sales	Last			Chg.	N.Y. Close
SP100	Jun345	75142	1½	−		⅝	345.87
SP100	Jun340	27473	6⅜	+		⅛	345.87
SP100	Jun350	15919	1-16	−		¼	345.87
SP100	Jul360	12920	1½	−		½	345.87
SP100	Jul345	12116	8	−		⅛	345.87

PUTS

		Sales	Last			Chg.	N.Y. Close
SP100	Jun345	62686	1-16	−	1⅛	345.87
SP100	Jun340	23485	1-16	−	¼	345.87
SP100	Jun350	16009	3½	−	⅞	345.87
SP100	Jul345	13810	4¾	−	⅞	345.87
SP100	Jul340	13738	3¼	−	⅝	345.87

AMERICAN

CALLS

		Sales	Last			Chg.	N.Y. Close
MMIdx	Jun585	14181	1⅛	−	3-16	586.14
Reebok	Oct20	7574	1⅜	+	⅜	18⅝
MMIdx	Jun580	6060	6	+	2⅛	586.14
MMIdx	Jul620	5278	1	−	¼	586.14
Disney	Jun130	5014	1½	+	⅞	131¾

PUTS

		Sales	Last			Chg.	N.Y. Close
MMIdx	Jun580	5434	1-16	−	1⅝	586.14
MMIdx	Jun575	4619	1-16	−	½	586.14
Ph Mor	Jun45	3720	1⅛	+	5-16	44
MMIdx	Jun585	2609	1-16	−4	3-16	586.14
Apple	Jun40	2591	½	+	¼	39½

PHILADELPHIA

CALLS

		Sales	Last			Chg.	N.Y. Close
F N M	Jun40	1494	1 9-16	−1	1-16	41⅝
Abbt L	Aug37½	1180	2 5-16	−	1-16	38⅝
F N M	Jul45	862	⅝	−	5-16	41⅝
McGHII	Jul55	761	2 11-16	+	7-16	56⅜
Waste	Jun40	756	13-16	−	1-16	40¾

PUTS

		Sales	Last			Chg.	N.Y. Close
UniTel	Jul40	608	1½	+	½	39⅞
F N M	Jul40	407	⅞	+	3-16	41⅝
SafKIn	Jul35	400	11-16	+	1-16	38⅛
Abbt L	Aug37½	315	1¼	+	⅛	38⅝
NwmtG	Jul40	303	3	−	½	38¼

PACIFIC

CALLS

		Sales	Last			Chg.	N.Y. Close
Wendy	Sep7½	3942	¾		....	6¾
Hilton	Jun55	3333	1 5-16	+	13-16	56¼
Compaq	Jun130	2947	1-16	−	5-16	128
Scher	Jun45	2550	1	−	⅞	45⅞
Scher	Jul45	2378	1⅞	−	⅛	45⅞

PUTS

		Sales	Last			Chg.	N.Y. Close
Mc D D	Aug40	706	3		....	38⅝
Hilton	Jul55	705	1 5-16	−	3-16	56¼
Compaq	Jul115	692	1¼	−	⅛	128
TCBY	Jul20	658	2½		....	18⅝
Compaq	Jul125	654	3⅜	−	¼	128

NEW YORK

CALLS

		Sales	Last			Chg.	N.Y. Close
CSoup	Jul65	4299	2 7-16		....	60⅝
CSoup	Jul60	2532	4	+	⅜	60⅝
ConFrt	Sep17½	1182	1 1-16	−	½	16¼
QntmCp	Jun22½	756	1-16	−	1-16	22½
Chubb	Jul45	750	3⅜	−	2⅛	47¾

PUTS

		Sales	Last			Chg.	N.Y. Close
Chubb	Jul45	750	5-16	−	1-16	47¾
ConFrt	Jun17½	432	1⅛	+	9-16	16¼
ConFrt	Sep20	405	4⅛	+	½	16¼
NY Idx	Aug200	220	5½	+	⅝	197.86
NY Idx	Jul200	216	4¼	+	13-16	197.86

Why not try index options.

As the managers concern is a *declining* market he has two choices:

Buy (long) index puts

Sell (write) index calls

If he buys an appropriate number of S&P 100 Stock Index puts with a strike price of 320, he will protect his portfolio. If the market drops, so will the value of the index. He can then sell the puts at a profit or exercise them and receive the cash difference. His only risk, as it is, with stock options, is the premium paid for the puts.

Or he might write S&P 100 calls with a 320 strike. If the market goes down, the calls will not be exercised, and the premium received would offset some of the damage done to the portfolio. The risk involved in this strategy is far greater, however, because if the market rises, the calls will be exercised against him. If the premium received is not sufficient to offset the loss upon exercise, his result will be negative. But he will have experienced an increase in the value of the portfolio. In all, he may have done quite well by using index options.

Let's look at another professional usage of index options. The manager of the endowment fund at Paper Mill University is faced with a problem. It is November, and she foresees a major upward market move in the immediate future. But she has no funds to invest, as the alumni have not been generous. It seems that Paper Mill lost 8 of its 10 football games this year including the final game to arch-rival Underachiever University by a score of 47-0.

How can she participate in the upcoming market really? Index options could provide the answer.

Our manager might purchase

S&P 100 Jan 320 Calls - Premium 3

If we presume that the value of this index is currently 312, she would participate in a market rally for a far smaller capital investment than would be needed to purchase the actual underlying stock.

At the time of purchase, each call would cost a premium of

$300. As the strike price is 320 the index would have to be at 323 at expiration for her to break-even.

Strike price	320
Plus premium	3
Break-even at expiration	323

If our portfolio manager was correct in her market analysis, as the S&P 100 Index rose to 330, her 320 calls would have an intrinsic value of 10 points ($1,000). After subtracting the $300 premium, she would have a $700 profit on each call.

But she'd better be right. If the index declines, her calls will expire worthless, and the entire premium will be lost.

But the availability of index options has enabled her to participate in the general movement of the market with a minimum outlay of cash. It has served as an alternative to the more traditional method of investing.

A few examples of the uses of index options have been provided. They are a very viable product which can be utilized by both individual and professional investors.

FOREIGN CURRENCY OPTIONS

The listing of equity options on the CBOE in 1973 opened the door for other new products. In 1982, the Philadelphia Stock Exchange introduced trading in options on foreign currencies. Sometime later, the CBOE also began trading in this product.

At the time of this writing, options are available on seven foreign currencies:

Australian dollars

British pounds

Canadian dollars

West German marks

French francs

Japanese Yen

Swiss Francs

Figure 10.2 shows that trading in these options is quite similar to that of equity options. Both puts and calls are available in each of three expiration months. The number of strike prices varies with the volatility of the underlying currency. Premiums are stated in U.S. dollars and cents.

Note that for each currency there are two listings. The first is traded in the usual manner, allowing the holder to exercise the option at any time prior to expiration. The second listing is for "European style" options which can only be exercised on the final day of the contract's life. This deprives the holder of the right to exercise during the life of the contract when the value of the underlying currency might be advantageous.

One difference between foreign currency options and equity options is the size of each contract. In an equity option each contract generally represents 100 shares of the underlying security. In currency options the contract size ranges from 31,250 British pounds to 6,250,000 Japanese yen. The contract size is dictated by the relationship of the value of the foreign currency to the U.S. dollar.

A British pound contract with an exercise price of 1.60 (U.S. $1.60) would have an aggregate value of $50,000 (31,250 British pounds × $1.60 = $50,000).

The premiums are expressed in cents-per-unit in the contract. Figure 10.2 indicates that the premium of the British pound June 170 call was 1.20 ($.0120).

Figure 10.2. Foreign Exchange Options

OPTIONS
PHILADELPHIA EXCHANGE

Option & Underlying	Strike Price	Calls—Last Jun	Jul	Sep	Puts—Last Jun	Jul	Sep
50,000 Australian Dollars-cents per unit.							
ADolr	...72	r	r	r	r	r	0.23
118.63	..75	2.64	r	r	r	r	r
118.63	..76	1.63	1.49	r	r	r	1.30
118.63	..77	0.66	r	r	r	r	r
118.63	..78	0.03	0.40	r	0.52	r	r
50,000 Australian Dollars-European Style.							
118.63	..77	0.61	r	r	r	r	r
31,250 British Pounds-cents per unit.							
BPound	162½	r	r	r	r	r	1.05
170.91	.165	6.15	5.30	r	r	r	r
170.91	167½	3.65	3.27	3.60	r	0.65	r
170.91	.170	1.20	1.88	2.40	0.15	1.70	r
170.91	172½	r	r	1.57	r	3.35	5.60
170.91	177½	r	s	0.67	r	s	r
31,250 British Pounds-European Style.							
170.91	.165	5.55	4.95	r	r	r	r
170.91	.170	1.33	r	r	r	r	r
50,000 Canadian Dollars-cents per unit.							
CDolr	.82½	r	r	r	r	0.05	0.30
85.34	.83½	r	r	r	r	0.11	r
85.34	..84	1.30	r	r	r	0.19	r
85.34	..85	0.38	0.42	r	0.01	r	1.34
85.34	.85½	r	r	0.44	0.20	r	r
85.34	..86	r	0.15	r	0.68	r	r
85.34	..87	r	0.05	r	r	r	r
50,000 Canadian Dollars-European Style.							
CDollar	..81	4.30	r	r	r	r	r
85.34	.83½	r	r	1.17	r	r	r
85.34	..84	r	r	r	r	0.17	r
85.34	.84½	r	r	r	r	0.28	r
85.34	..85	0.37	0.41	r	r	0.44	r
85.34	.85½	0.02	0.20	r	r	r	r
62,500 West German Marks-cents per unit.							
DMark	.. 55	r	r	r	r	r	0.14
59.23	...57	r	r	r	r	0.09	r
59.23	.57½	r	r	s	r	0.17	s
59.23	...58	1.00	1.33	r	r	0.20	0.71
59.23	.58½	0.34	r	s	0.01	0.38	s
59.23	...59	0.27	0.75	s	0.01	0.50	r
59.23	.59½	0.02	r	s	0.22	0.80	s
59.23	...60	0.01	0.26	0.72	0.78	r	r
59.23	.60½	0.01	r	s	1.48	r	s
59.23	...61	r	0.10	0.54	1.78	r	2.58
59.23	.61½	r	r	s	2.47	r	s
62,500 West German Marks-European Style.							
59.23	...54	5.10	5.04	4.77	r	r	r
59.23	...58	r	r	r	r	0.34	r
59.23	.59½	r	r	s	0.47	r	s
59.23	...60	0.02	r	r	r	r	r
250,000 French Francs-10ths of a cent per unit.							
FFranc	15½	20.38	r	r	r	r	r
250,000 French Francs-European Style.							
175.74	15½	20.38	r	r	r	r	r
6,250,000 Japanese Yen-100ths of a cent per unit.							
JYen	... 60	r	r	r	r	r	0.07
64.96	...64	0.78	r	r	0.01	0.32	r
64.96	.64½	0.40	0.83	s	0.05	r	s
64.96	...65	0.04	0.55	r	0.07	0.59	1.18
64.96	.65½	0.02	r	s	0.60	r	s
64.96	...66	0.01	0.28	0.64	1.04	r	r
64.96	.66½	0.02	r	s	r	r	s
64.96	...67	r	0.12	r	r	r	r
64.96	...68	r	0.05	r	r	r	r
64.96	...69	r	0.02	0.14	r	r	r
64.96	...70	r	r	r	4.97	r	r
6,250,000 Japanese Yen-European Style.							
64.96	...69	r	r	r	4.16	4.06	r
62,500 Swiss Francs-cents per unit.							
SFranc	..66	3.77	r	r	r	r	r
69.81	...67	2.95	r	r	r	0.11	r
69.81	...68	1.95	r	r	r	0.26	r
69.81	.68½	r	r	s	r	0.40	s
69.81	...69	0.95	r	r	0.04	r	r
69.81	.69½	0.33	0.85	r	0.07	0.60	s
69.81	...70	0.02	r	r	0.25	r	r
69.81	.70½	0.06	r	r	0.70	r	s
69.81	...71	r	0.33	r	r	r	r
69.81	.71½	r	r	r	1.70	r	s
62,500 European Currency Units-cents per unit.							
ECU	122	r	r		r	0.44	r

Total call vol. 29,388   Call open int. 411,874
Total put vol. 33,674   Put open int. 438,833
r—Not traded. s—No option offered.
Last is premium (purchase price).

If you purchased one of these calls the cost of the option would be $375.00 (31,250 pounds times $.0120 equals $375.00). The call allows you to purchase pounds at $1.70 each. As you paid a premium of .0120 your break-even point in March would be $171.20.

If, at expiration, the British pound was worth U.S. $178, you could exercise your contract at $1.70 and, including the premium cost, purchase 31,250 pounds for a total cost of $50,828.13.

Exercise Price: 1.70 × 31,250 = $53,125.00
Premium: $.0120 × 31250 = 375.00
Total cost $53,500.00

If you then sold the pounds at $1.78 each, your proceeds would be $55,625.00 giving you a profit of $2,125.00.

Sale price of British pounds ($1.78) = $55,625.00
Exercise cost plus premium   = 53,500.00
Profit $ 2,125.00

Foreign currency options can be applied in much the same way as equity options. They can be used to speculate on movements of other currencies against the U.S. dollar, and they can be used to protect positions. These options are used by business people to insure against losses on transactions due to currency fluctuation.

EXAMPLE:

You are an American manufacturer of basketballs. You have sold a substantial number of balls to a West German client. You expect payment in about 30 days, but payment will be made in West German marks not U.S. dollars. When the order was shipped, the German mark was worth U.S. $.59, and your selling price was based on that comparative value.

Suppose before payment is made, the value of the mark drops to 52 cents. Your profit on the sale would certainly be lower and could possibly disappear.

What can you do?

One solution would be to purchase puts on the West German mark.

You purchase:

West German mark Jan 60 Puts - Premium $.01.

Your price is now protected. If the mark declines to 52 cents you can exercise your put and sell at 60 cents. When you subtract the 1 cent premium, your net price is 59 cents per mark. This is the value on which your order was based, so all is well.

If the mark were to increase in value to 63 cents you would fare even better. You had a profit with marks at 59 cents. That profit will be far better if the value on receipt is 63 cents. Even allowing for the 1 cent premium paid for the put, you net 62 cents per mark rather than the 59 cents value at the time your order was shipped.

The introduction of options on foreign currencies has enabled international banks and multinational corporations to conveniently protect themselves against market uncertainties which can be caused by financial or political events.

INTEREST RATE OPTIONS

Options are also available on three types of securities issued by the U.S. Treasury:

Treasury bills (American Stock Exchange)

Treasury notes (American Stock Exchange and CBOE)

Treasury bonds (CBOE)

Just as we have noted with index options and currency options, there are many similarities in Treasury options and equity options trading.

Both puts and calls are available, and the three expiration months and options strike prices are established by the exchange on which the contract trades.

A contract for Treasury bills represents $1 million face value of 13-week bills.

Treasury note and Treasury bond contracts represent $100,000 face value of the underlying securities which have longer maturities.

Large investors can use these options to speculate on changes in interest rates or to protect large bond positions.

A pension fund with a large portfolio of Treasury securities can hedge against lower prices by purchasing puts or by writing calls against the portfolio.

Values of U.S. Treasury securities are generally expressed as the yield provided by the instrument to the investor.

An 8% Treasury bond trading at a price below face value ($1,000) would be said to be trading at a discount. As the stated rate of 8% does not change, the actual return or yield to the investor would be greater than 8%. This security might be trading at an "8.20 basis." This means the actual return at the current price is 8.20%, somewhat larger than the stated rate of 8%.

If the price of the bond were above the face value, the bond would be trading at a "premium." The yield might be only 7.90%.

As interest rates rise, the values of outstanding bonds decline to reflect the now-higher returns. Conversely, if interest rates decline, outstanding bonds will move to higher levels to bring the yield to the investor in line with the rates current in the market.

Investors can use interest-rate options to speculate on or

protect against these changes, just as equity options are used to cushion the effect of price changes on the underlying stock.

A total study of index options, currency options, or interest rate options would require a complete and detailed book. Our intention here is merely to bring these products to the reader's attention.

But one point is clear. No matter what the option is based on—stocks, indexes, currencies, or interest rates, there are only two types—puts and calls. They are used in the same manner and for the same purposes no matter what underlying product they represent.

MARGIN REQUIREMENTS

In many ways, the margin requirements under Federal Reserve Regulation T for index, currency, and interest rate options are the same as those for equity options which were covered in Chapter 9. But because of the basic difference in these products, such as contract size and method of settlement, some variations can be found. A brief look at these requirements will be helpful to those considering investing in these contracts.

Purchases

The purchase of an option to create a long position requires the payment of 100% of the premium. This is true of all options products.

Index Options

Buy 1 OEX JUN 345 Call - Premium 6¼

OEX is the symbol used to identify the Standard and Poor's 100 stock index options. To determine the amount of premium we use a multiplier which is $100 for index options. Each point of premium is valued at $100 so the total margin required for this purchase is $625.

$$\text{Multiplier} \times \text{Premium} = \text{Total}$$
$$\$100 \times 6\frac{1}{4} = \$625$$

Currency Options. Currency options vary in size depending on the relative value of each nation's monetary unit to the U.S. dollar. A table of currency options traded on the Philadelphia Stock Exchange together with the size of each contract can be found earlier in this chapter in Figure 10.2.

Note that the British pound contract represents 31,250 pounds. The premium is quoted in cents per unit.

Buy 1 XBP JUN 167½ Call - Premium 2.20

The purchaser now has an option to purchase 31,250 British pounds at $1.67½ each until expiration in June. The premium paid was $.0220 per unit.

The contract size is multiplied by the premium to determine the amount of margin required.

$$\text{Contract size} \times \text{Premium} = \text{Total}$$
$$31{,}250 \times \$.0220 = \$687.50$$

The total amount of the premium, $687.50, would be required. Although Federal Reserve Regulation T allows seven business days for payment to be accomplished, most firms would demand payment much sooner, perhaps even prior to the order being executed. This is a result of the OCC rule which requires the broker to pay for options on the first business day after purchase. The firms do not wish to be advancing their own funds.

Interest rate Options. The contract on interest rate options for U.S. Treasury securities is $1 million for Treasury bills and $100,000 for Treasury notes and bonds. Premiums are quoted in points which represent 1% of $1,000, or $10 per point fractions of a point are quoted in 1/32 of a point: A premium of 3.12 equals 3¹²/₃₂ of a point or $33.75 per unit (3 points equals $30 plus ¹²/₃₂ or ⅜ of $10 which equals $3.75).

Therefore a premium of 3.12 paid to purchase one U.S. Treasury note contract would require a deposit of $3,375. As the premium is $33.75 per thousand and as there are 100 units of $1,000 in each contract we compute as follows:

Units per contract × Premium = Total
100   × $33.75   = $3,375

Covered Writing

As is the case with equity options, no margin is required to write a covered option or indexes, currencies, or interest rates.

In the case of index options, settlement is made in cash not in the underlying product. For this reason only a properly executed bank escrow agreement would provide cover for writing these contracts.

Uncovered Writing

To write an uncovered option on any of the products under discussion the same formula is used as with equity options.

Percentage of market value + Premium − Out of the money amount

Although the formula is the same, the percentages used vary among the products. Again, as with equity options there is a minimum requirement that applies in all situations. Although the percentages will vary, the formula is consistent.

Table 10.1. Standard Margin Requirement

	Premium Plus % of Market Value
Broad based index	15%
Narrow based index	20%
Foreign currency	4%
Treasury bills	.35%
Treasury notes	3%
Treasury bonds	3.5%

Percentage of market value + Premium

One further distinction is made in the case of index options. They are divided into two categories and each has different requirements. The divisions are Broad Based Index and Narrow Based Index.

A "broad based index" has many components which represent a variety of industries. A "narrow based index" includes securities within a single particular industry.

Tables 10.1 and 10.2 demonstrate both the standard and minimum margin requirements for these products.

In all calculations in Table 10.1, the out of the money amount, if any, may be subtracted from this total.

In all cases, there is a minimum requirement which consists of the premium plus an appropriate percentage of the market value.

Table 10.2. Minimum Margin Requirements

	Premium Plus % of Market Value
Broad based index	10%
Narrow based index	10%
Foreign currency	¾%
Treasury bills	¹⁄₂₀%
Treasury notes	½%
Treasury bonds	½%

Since January 1986, the basic requirements have been determined by the exchanges on which the options are traded and by the National Association of Securities Dealers. The decisions of these self-regulatory bodies are subject to the approval of the SEC. The requirements can be changed at any time should market conditions so dictate.

Individual brokerage firms often impose higher requirements to protect themselves from risk. Your broker will be pleased to supply you with the details of any "house rules."

Summary

In the course of our study of equity options, we have looked at the potential risks and rewards of various strategies. As this is an investor's most important concern, it would do us well to list these possibilities again.

LONG OPTIONS POSITIONS

Potential Risks

The buyer of equity options takes on the risk of losing the entire amount paid in premiums. It makes no difference if one buys puts, calls, straddles, or combinations, the entire amount expended can be lost. Although the degree of risk may vary, straddles for instance present less risk of an entire loss of premium, *the possible loss is absolute.*

Those who use long options positions should be financially and psychologically prepared to assume this risk.

If an investor wishes to speculate on a rise in the price of XYZ stock by purchasing a call on that stock for a premium of 3, he must realize that the entire premium can be forfeited.

His reasoning must be similar to spending a pleasant day at the races with his spouse. They predetermine that they can afford to lose $300 without damage to their budget. If they lose, they are still able to pay their bills. If by chance they win, the joy of the day is enhanced. However, if the $300 is earmarked for next week's household expenses, they would be better advised to stay at home and watch television.

In purchasing 1 ABZ Oct 60 put for a premium of 6 and at expiration ABZ stock is trading at 57, your put is in the money by 3 points. You might sell it at that price and reduce your loss to $300. But loss of the entire $600 represents the maximum loss you could suffer.

Long options positions also have another feature which works against the holder. Options expire. From time of purchase the investor usually has only a few months to be proven correct. While an option is still trading, its value is unlimited. When it expires it is worthless.

Potential Rewards

The potential rewards of buying equity options are most tempting. In some cases, such as long calls, long straddles, and long combinations, the profit potential is unlimited. As each of these strategies gives the holder the right to purchase (call) a stock at a fixed price, no maximum figure can be placed on how much money can be made.

If you own a call on IBM with a strike price of 105, you have the privilege of purchasing stock at $105 a share. How high up can IBM stock go? $150, $200, $300, $1,000 a share? There may be no limit.

A long put position offers potential for a large profit but the maximum possibility is measurable.

If you purchase an ABZ Dec 90 put for a premium of 4, you could have a profit of $8,600. Your cost for the put was $400. The option gives you the right to sell stock at 90 ($9,000). If ABZ stock becomes worthless, you might acquire it at a cost of 0 and sell (put) it at 90. The result is a profit of $8,600.

It is this huge potential for profit that gives long option positions an aura of glamour that may not be deserved. These huge profits can, of course, occur but they are rare. In many states a lottery is held each week offering prizes that run to many millions of dollars. We all dream of winning the big prize but are intelligent enough to know what little chance we have. While long options positions are not entirely comparable to lottery tickets, the possible result is the same. If you win you may win big. If you lose, the loss can be total.

WRITING OPTIONS

Potential Risk

The risk involved in writing options depends upon the writer's position. If she is a covered writer, her risk is limited. If she writes uncovered options, the potential loss in some cases cannot be measured.

Covered Call Writing

Let's look again at an example of a covered call. A client purchases 100 shares of Dow Chemical stock at $92 a share.
Later she writes.

1 Dow Jan 95 Call for a premium of 4

She has protected herself on the stock she purchased. If Dow went down and she sold it at $88 a share she would be even. The 4-point loss on the stock (purchased at $92) is offset by the 4-point premium received for writing the call. Naturally, if Dow drops below 88, she will lose. But she has protected her position to some degree.

This strategy has reduced her potential profit but cannot truly be defined as risk.

Should Dow stock rise to $110 a share, she will be called at 95. When we add the 4-point premium that she received, her sale price is actually $99 a share. When we compare this to her cost of 92, a 7-point profit has resulted. Had she not written the call, she would still own it and could sell at $110 a share for an 18-point profit. So she made $700 by writing the call and would have made $1,800 had she not established the position. But a reasonable profit was recorded, and the call protected her had the stock declined in value.

Uncovered Writing

We have stated earlier that an uncovered option writer assumes tremendous risk. If he writes an uncovered call, this risk is unlimited. The uncovered put writer can lose an amount equal to the aggregate exercise price of the put minus the premium received.

Write one XYZ Sept 90 Put - Premium 7. If the stock falls to 0 the loss is $8,300.

Aggregate exercise price (90):	$9,000
Premium received	700
Potential loss	$8,300

Uncovered option writers have a limited potential profit.

All they can make is the premium. If the call is not exercised against the writer, it expires and the premium is retained.

Although uncovered writing is a factor in many option strategies, it should be reserved for professional investors and traders.

Individual investors may be able to afford the potential loss of premium that could result from purchasing options. They might even find covered writing a useful tool in protecting positions and earning extra income.

But uncovered writing is not suitable for most individuals. Some may have the financial ability to assume such risks, but for most it is a market technique that should be understood but not applied.

ALTERNATIVE PORTFOLIOS

The investing attitudes of investors are as varied as is their taste for food. Investor Brown lives on Mexican food prepared with a double order of the hottest sauce. Investor Jones dines strictly on meat and potatoes, while investor Smith exists solely on health food salads and wheat germ. So too, would be the variety of their appetites for investing.

Suppose Brown, Jones, and Smith each had $10,000 to invest. Each of them is optimistic about the possibilities of XYZ common stock. XYZ is trading at $50 a share and paying a $4 annual dividend. Each of the three phones his or her broker and makes the following investments:

Brown

    Buys 200 shares of XYZ at $50 a share

Jones

    Buys 100 shares of XYZ at $50 a share

    Buys 20 XYZ Aug 50 Calls - Premium 2½

Smith

Buys $10,000 U.S. Treasury 8% Notes at PAR

Brown feels strongly about the potential for XYZ stock so he buys 200 shares. He feels the stock is a good long-term holding and the $4 dividend provides an annual return of 8%. He knows the stock might decline in value resulting in a loss, but he is willing to take that risk.

Jones feels that XYZ will rise in price in the immediate future. She puts only half her money in the stock and uses the balance to purchase the calls. If she is correct the value of the calls will increase sharply. If she is wrong she will have a problem, but this risk is suitable to her financial and emotional condition.

Smith also likes XYZ stock but avoids any investment that entails risk. As both common stock and options carry varying degrees of risk, he shuns both of them and contents himself with the low-risk investment in U.S. Treasury notes.

Suppose that six months later the XYZ calls expire, and the U.S. Treasury notes mature. XYZ stock has paid two quarterly dividends of $1 a share.

How did our three investors fare? That depends on the price of XYZ stock at the end of the six months.

Tables 11.1 through 11.3 look at *three* possibilities that could exist at the time the XYZ calls expired.

Table 11.1 shows us that *Smith's* conservative approach brought about the best results as XYZ stock declined, and the call options expired worthless.

As Table 11.2 shows us, *Brown* benefited by the slight increase in the price of XYZ stock and continued to receive dividends. While the XYZ Aug 50 calls had an intrinsic value of 1 point at expiration, it was still well below Jones' cost of 2½. Smith still had his annualized 8% return without risk.

Table 11.1. XYZ Stock at $44 a Share ($10,000 Invested)

Brown		Jones		Smith	
200 shares XYZ @ 44	$8,800	100 shares XYZ	$4,400	$10,000 Treasury notes	$10,000
Dividends ($2.00 per share)	400	Dividends	200	Interest (six months)	400
		20 XYZ calls	0		
Total value	$9,200		$4,600		$10,400

Table 11.2. XYZ Stock at $51 a Share ($10,000 Invested)

Brown		Jones		Smith	
200 shares XYZ	$10,200	100 shares XYZ	$5,100	U.S. Treasury notes	$10,000
Dividends	400	Dividends	200	Interest (six months)	400
		20 XYZ calls	2,000		
Total value	$10,600		$7,300		$10,400

Table 11.3. XYZ Stock at $56 a Share ($10,000 Invested)

Brown		Jones		Smith	
200 shares XYZ	$11,200	100 shares XYZ	$5,600	U.S. Treasury notes	$10,000
Dividends	400	Dividends	200	Interest (six months)	400
		20 XYZ calls	12,000		
Total value	$11,600		$17,800		$10,400

At expiration, as Table 11.3 shows, the XYZ Aug 50 calls had an intrinsic value of 6 points on $600 each. This helped to drive Jones' original $10,000 investment to $17,800.

Although Jones was clearly a winner as seen in Table 11.3, we must remember that she was a big loser in Tables 11.1 and 11.2. Brown has a very satisfactory return on his 200 shares of XYZ and still owns the stock. Smith will probably buy some more U.S. Treasury securities, accept a trouble-free return, and never suffer from an ulcer.

Our examples were constructed to compare options to more conservative investments. It is apparent that in most situations the purchase of options can result in very large gains or losses. Each investor must decide independently to what degree, if any, this product fits into his portfolio.

In periods of major market disruption, the effect on options can be dramatic. On Wednesday, October 15, 1987, the Dow Jones Industrial Average closed at 2412.70. Three business days later, on Monday, October 19, 1987, the Dow closed at 1738.74 a decline over this short period of 673.96 or approximately 28%. The effect of this drop was even more pronounced on equity options, as Saturday, October 17, was the expiration date for the October puts and calls. This led to some highly unusual situations. Some were profitable others were nearly disastrous. Let's look at a few examples.

Suppose a client had purchased an IBM Oct 130 call. On the last trading day for that option, Friday, October 16, 1987, IBM stock closed at 134½. The call would have been automatically exercised, and the owner would have purchased 100 shares of IBM at 130 plus whatever premium she had paid. Two business days later on October 19, IBM stock closed at 103¼. On paper she would have a loss of 26¾ points plus the premium paid.

But suppose on Thursday, October 15 she had purchased an IBM Nov 140 put at its closing premium of 6. By the close of business on the following Tuesday, the premium for that same put was 32, more than five times her cost a few days earlier.

An even more vivid example would be the performance of Teledyne stock. On Thursday, October 15, the closing price was 362¼. On Tuesday, October 20, the Teledyne shares closed at 270, down a total of 92¼ points in five business days. Many holders of calls or writers of puts suffered major losses.

However, suppose you had bought some Teledyne Jan 350 puts on Thursday, October 15. The closing premium on that day was 4¾. By the close of the business on the following Tuesday, the premium had risen to 77, and these puts had an intrinsic value of 80 points. The purchaser of Teledyne puts was planning a fine winter vacation. The writer of these same puts had suffered a severe financial loss.

The reaction to such market variations would depend on which side of the market you were on.

If you were on the upside long calls or short puts, you were devastated. If you were on the downside long puts or short calls, you recorded major profits.

The market eventually recovered from the October, 1987 decline and on Thursday, October 12, 1989, the Dow Jones Industrial Average stood at 2759.84. On the following day, Friday, October 13, the Dow dropped 190.58 points to 2569.26. Table 11.4 looks at some closing prices of options on those two days.

Table 11.4. Some Options Price Closings, October 12–13, 1989

	10/12/89	10/13/89
S&P 100 Index - Oct 330 Call	3½	½
S&P 100 Index - Oct 330 Put	2¼	12
IBM Jan 110 Call	4	2⅝
IBM Jan 110 Put	5⅜	11
Disney Dec 130 Call	13	6
Disney Dec 130 Put	4	12¼

Those who used options to speculate had good or bad results depending on which side of the market they chose.

Those who used them to protect positions, however, had some amount of success in any case.

If a client was long stock and had purchased puts to protect his position, he would not have been seriously hurt by the decline in 1987 or in 1989. Even if he had written calls, the premium received would have protected him against the decline to some degree.

Had a client been short stock and purchased calls, the premium would have been lost, but she would have profited on her short position. Had she written puts, they would probably have been exercised against her. This would have covered her short sale, and she would have retained the premium received.

Options are a varied and most interesting product. They have virtually unlimited applications in the world of investing. In some cases they can be the medicine needed to solve a problem, but they can often be dangerous to your health. It would not be incorrect to compare options to human beings. They have many similar characteristics.

There are two divisions of humans, male and female. There are two divisions of options, puts and calls.

Each human, male or female, has individual characteristics. Each option is unique from each other. We call these "series" of options.

Human behavior is often unpredictable. The behavior of option premiums has baffled even the experts.

But the most important characteristic that humans and options share is that eventually, they both expire.

Equity Options—Equivalent Positions

There is often more than one way to accomplish a desired goal. If your doctor advised you to eliminate salt from your diet it would not be a crushing blow, but it certainly would reduce the joy when you eat that sweet summer corn on the cob. What is corn without salt and butter? But science comes to the rescue. You find that there are doctor-approved substitutes for both of the desired additives. Or, you're driving to work and the bridge is closed for repairs; you drive a few miles south and use the tunnel instead. It's a different route, but you do get across the river. Dealing in equity options also offers alternate choices which are called *equivalent positions*. They are much the same as a synthetic product created to replace the real thing.

For each type of option, put or call, there are two possible positions, long or short. We have studied the basic uses of these positions earlier. Briefly, a client who believes that the value of a security will rise in price could profit from this outcome by using two options positions: long calls and short puts. These positions cover the *upside* of the market. An anticipated decline in a stock's value, the *downside*, could be represented by the two opposite positions: long puts and short calls.

Each of these four equity options positions is taken to achieve a desired goal. However, in each case there is a substitute, an equivalent position, which will entail the same risks and offer the same potential for profits. We will look at an example of each of these equivalents and demonstrate the fact that while the components are different, the investment results would be the same.

1. Long call equals long stock and long put

Client Jones looks for the price of Motorola Inc. to increase from its current value of $75 a share. To participate in this increase he executes the following order:

Buy 1 MOT Oct 75 Call—Premium 5

The maximum possible loss from this position is $500, the amount of premium paid. If Motorola declines in value, the option will expire unexercised and Jones will forfeit the premium. But the loss cannot exceed $500.

The potential profit from owning this call is unlimited. If Jones exercises the option, the stock is purchased at $80 a share. Any higher price represents a profit the extent of which cannot be measured. But, Jones can achieve the same results if, instead, he executed these orders:

Buy 1 MOT Oct 75 Put — Premium 5

Buy 100 shares MOT stock @ $75 a share

Again, the maximum loss is the $500 premium paid for the put option. If Motorola declines in price, Jones will exercise the put and sell his long stock position at $75 a share. This is a break-even proposition since $75 was the cost of the shares. His $500 premium is the price he must pay for being wrong.

However, the potential profit is unlimited. Jones owns 100 shares of Motorola stock. there is no limit as to how far the price can rise.

In either case, the results are the same. Maximum profit is unlimited, maximum loss equals $500.

2. Short put equals long stock and short call

The stock of Dresser Industries looks good to client Brown. She envisions higher prices ahead. She places the following order:

Sell (write) 1 DI Sep 45 Put — Premium 4

She receives the $400 premium; this represents her maximum potential for profit should Dresser stock, in fact, rise in value. If the shares are selling at $49 a share on expiration in October, the put will not be exercised against her. No one would sell her stock at $45 a share when the actual market value is $49 a share. Therefore, she keeps the $400, but the position could result in a loss as large as $4,100. Suppose Dresser shares became worthless. The put would be exercised against her and she would be required to buy 100 shares at $45 a share ($4,500). As the stock is without value, her loss would be $4,100 because she did receive the $400 premium for writing the put.

For the same possible results, Brown could execute these orders:

Buy 100 shares of DI @ $45 a share

Sell (write) 1 DI Sep 45 Call—Premium 4

Dresser Industries' stock goes up to $52 a share and the 45 call is exercised against her. But she is long the stock and delivers the shares when called; no loss occurs. She profits from the $400 premium received for writing the call.

Again, she still risks the loss of as much as $4,100. Dresser shares could become worthless and poor Brown owns 100 shares for which she paid $4,500. Her only solace is the $400 premium she received. In both cases, the potential result from either position was the same. Maximum profit is $400, maximum loss equals $4,100.

3. Long put equals short stock and long call

If client Smith thought Pepsi Co. Inc. stock, which is trading at $80 a share, was due for a fall, he might purchase a put option on the stock.

Buy 1 PEP Jan 80 Put — Premium 3 ½

His total investment is $350, the cost of the option. If he was mistaken, and the PEP stock rises in value, he loses the $350; but, the profit possibility is much greater. At expiration in January, PEP stock has dropped to $70 a share. Smith could purchase 100 shares at 70 and, by exercising his put, sell the stock at $80. The gross profit of $1,000 is reduced by the $350 premium paid, leaving him a net gain of $650.

On the other hand, suppose the PEP Jan 80 put is not offered for sale in the market. Smith could create the same situation by executing these orders:

Sell 100 shares PEP stock @ $80 a share short

Buy 1 PEP Jan 80 Call — Premium 3 ½

Smith is now short 100 shares at $80 and long 1 PEP Jan 80 call at a cost of $350. But let's again suppose that Smith was wrong. PEP stock rises. He exercises his call at 80 and covers the short sale made at the same price. He now has no position, but has recorded a loss of $350.

What if Smith was an excellent forecaster of the market? PEP drops to $70 a share. He purchases 100 shares at that price and covers the short sale made at 80. The $1,000 profit is again reduced by the $350 paid out in premium. Net gain $650.

It is possible for either position to produce as much as $7,650 in profit. In the unlikely situation that Pepsi Co. stock drops to zero, both the long put or the short stock position would be worth $8,000. In each case, we would reduce this by the $350 premium cost, leaving a net of $7,650.

4. Short call equals short stock and short put

CBS stock, now selling at $180, is due for a decline. Or so thinks investor Green. She enjoys dealing in options as a method of implementing her market theories, so she executes the following order:

Sell (write) 1 CBS Nov 180 Call — Premium 10

The premium received for writing this call may seem high as the option has no intrinsic value. Both the market price of the stock and the strike price of the call are the same, 180. But Green writes the call in August. Since it does not expire until November, there are approximately three months of life left in the call. Because CBS stock is quite volatile, this premium is not at all out of line. Buyers of options pay high prices for contracts on volatile stocks with long periods of time remaining.

Green's objective is to make $1,000, the premium received for her short sale of the option. She will succeed if the stock is below $180 at expiration. At any such price, the contract will not be exercised against her and she keeps the $1,000. Should CBS be at $183 at expiration, she will be called at 180 and required to deliver the stock at that price. Should she buy the shares in the open market at $183 and sell at $180, she loses $300 on the transaction; but remember, she had $1,000 of premium in her pocket. Her profit is reduced to $700, but she still shows a gain. In any case, her maximum profit for writing this call would be $1,000.

However, her potential for loss is unlimited. Should CBS be above $190 a share at expiration, Green is a loser. With the $1,000 premium she could purchase as high as $190, deliver at $180 and break-even. Should CBS be at $200, $250, or $300 a share, she will suffer severely. Since *up* has no ceiling, she can lose an undeterminable amount.

By writing this call she had a potential profit of $1,000 and an unlimited possible loss.

Green may have created the same picture by using the equivalent position. She would execute these orders:

Sell 100 shares CBS @ 180 Short

Sell (write) 1 CBS Nov 180 Put — Premium 10

Again, she receives $1,000 in premium, this time for writing the put. If, as she suspected, CBS drops to $165 a share, the put will be exercised and she must purchase 100 shares at $180. But this simply covers her short sale made at that same price. No profit or loss results and she retains the $1,000 premium.

Still, the loss on this position could reach any amount. she is short CBS stock at $180 a share. If the value of these shares rises to $190 and she covers the short at that price, her loss is $1,000. Because the put that she wrote at a 180 strike price will not be exercised against her, the $1,000 premium will offset the loss on the short sale and she will break-even. Any price above $190 a share for CBS will cost her money. How much money we cannot compute. The possible loss is not measurable.

As with the sale of the call, this equivalent position offers the same potential. Maximum profit is $1,000, maximum loss is unlimited.

When evaluating equivalent positions, we must look beyond the raw numbers that were used in our examples. We have shown only the profit and loss potentials and by this standard alone, the positions are, in fact, equivalent. But in most cases, the expenses involved are not the same. When a client purchases or writes an equity option, it involves a single transaction; hence, only one commission is paid to the broker handling the transaction. Equivalents entail two transactions; the purchase or sale of the option, and the purchase or short sale of the underlying security. In almost all cases, this will result in the broker charging two separate commissions. In addition, when the strategy consists only of the purchase or sale of an option, the amount of money required will be less than that required for the equivalent position.

When you purchase a put or a call you are only required to deposit the premium paid.

When you write an uncovered put or call, the margin requirement is 20% of the market value plus the premium. This would then be adjusted for any out of the money amount.

The equivalents also contain a second element. In addition to paying for the option purchased or providing margin for the option written, we must consider the stock position (long or short) that is part of the package. If stock is purchased, it must be paid for. Even if the client buys on margin, his minimum deposit is 50%, much greater than that for writing uncovered options. Also, if margin is used to purchase the stock, the client borrows the additional amount from his broker. He will be charged interest on this loan.

If the equivalent includes a short sale of the stock, the client must deposit 50% of the proceeds of the sale in his margin account.

Let's look at our last example in which we used CBS and compare the possible costs involved.

SHORT CALL

Sell (write) 1 CBS Nov 180 Call — Premium 10

(CBS is trading at $180 a share.)

MARGIN REQUIREMENT

20% of Market Value ($18,000)	=	$3,600.00
Plus Premium		1,000.00
Total:		$4,600.00

(Because the option is at the money no adjustment is made.)

The client would be required to deposit $3,600 and would not be permitted to withdraw the $1,000 premium. He would be charged a commission by his broker for the sale of the call.

EQUIVALENT POSITION

Sell 100 Share CBS @ 180 Short

Sell 1 CBS Nov 180 Put — Premium 10

Margin on Short Sale = $9,000.00
(50% of sale proceeds)

MARGIN ON SALE OF PUT

20% of Market Value ($18,000)	=	$3,600.00
Plus Premium		1,000.00
Total:		$4,600.00

The customer would be required to deposit $9,000 as margin for the short sale of the stock and $3,600 for writing the uncovered put. This total of $12,600 is far greater than the $3,600 deposit needed to sell the uncovered call. In addition, the client will be charged separate commissions for each transaction.

So, these positions are not exactly equivalent when all factors are considered, but they do get the job done. In most cases, the equivalent position would only be used if the desired option was not available. It might be better if they were called *substitute positions* rather than *equivalent*. After all, those substitutes for butter and salt that you put on the corn really don't taste as good as the real thing, do they?

Listed Equity Options—
The Underlying Securities

The five exchanges on which equity options are traded provide markets for contracts on approximately 500 underlying stocks. Most of the stocks on which options are traded are listed on stock exchanges, such as the New York Stock Exchange and the American Stock Exchange. Some underlying stocks, however, are traded in the over-the-counter market. In the list that follows, the OTC stocks can be easily identified by the symbol which is used on quotation machines. Stocks listed on exchanges have symbols that do not exceed three characters (e.g., IBM = International Business Machines), while over-the-counter stocks are assigned symbols of four or more characters (e.g., Apple Computer = AAPL).

The list will also include the exchange on which each option is listed and the trading cycle in which each contract can be found. The following abbreviations will be used:

EXCHANGES:

A	=	American Stock Exchange
C	=	Chicago Board Options Exchange
N	=	New York Stock Exchange
P	=	Pacific Stock Exchange
Ph	=	Philadelphia Stock Exchange

(*Note*: Options on some securities are traded on more than one exchange.)

CYCLES:

J	=	January cycle
F	=	February cycle
M	=	March cycle

Symbol	Company	Cycle	Exchange
ABT	Abbott Laboratories	F	Ph
ACN	Acuson Corp.	J	P
ADBE	Adobe Systems	J	P
AMD	Advanced Micro Devices	J	P
AET	Aetna Life & Casualty	J	A
AFP	Affiliated Publications	J	C
AHM	Ahmanson & Co.	J	A
APD	Air Products & Chemicals	M	Ph
ALK	Alaska Air Group	J	A

Symbol	Company	Cycle	Exchange
ABS	Albertson's Inc.	M	Ph
AL	Alcan Aluminum	M	A
ASN	Alco Standard Corp.	M	N
AA	Alcoa	J	C
AAL	Alexander & Alexander	F	C
ALEX	Alexander & Baldwin	J	A
ALD	Allied Signal	M	Ph
AZA	ALZA Corp.	J	P
AMX	Amax Inc.	M	A
AMH	Amdahl Inc.	F	C
AHC	Amerada Hess	F	Ph
ABX	American Barrick Resources	J	A
AMB	American Brands	M	A
ACY	American Cyanamid	J	A
AEP	American Electric Power	F	C
AXP	American Express	J	A & C
AFL	American Family	F	A
AGC	American General	J	C
AGREA	American Greetings	J	C
AHP	American Home Products	J	A
AIG	American International Group	F	C
AMI	American Medical International	M	P
APS	American President Companies	J	P
ASC	American Stores	J	C
AIT	Ameritech	J	C
AMGN	Amgen Inc.	J	A
AN	Amoco Corp.	F	C
AMP	AMP Inc.	F	C
AMR	AMR Corp.	F	A
APC	Anadarko Petroleum	F	C
ADI	Analog Devices	M	Ph
BUD	Anheuser-Busch	M	Ph
APCI	Apollo Computer	J	A
AAPL	Apple Computer	J	A & C
ABIO	Applied Biosystems	J	P
APM	Applied Magnetics Corp.	M	C
ADM	Archer-Daniels-Midland	M	Ph
RCM	Arco Chemical Co.	J	A

Symbol	Company	Cycle	Exchange
ARS	Aristech Chemical	M	A
ALG	Arkla Inc.	F	Ph
AS	Armco Inc.	F	Ph
ACK	Armco World Industries	M	Ph
ASA	ASA Limited	F	A
AR	ASARCO Inc.	F	A
ASH	Ashland Oil	J	Ph
TATE	Ashton Tate	J	P
ARC	Atlantic Richfield	J	C
T	AT&T	J	C
ACAD	Autodesk	J	P
AUD	Automatic Data	F	Ph
AVY	Avery International	J	Ph
AVT	Avnet Inc.	F	A
AVP	Avon Products	J	C
BHI	Baker Hughes	J	P
BLY	Bally Manufacturing	F	A & C
ONE	Banc One Corp.	F	P
BKB	Bank of Boston	F	Ph
BK	Bank of New York	J	C
BAC	BankAmerica Corp.	J	C
BT	Bankers Trust N.Y.	J	P
BCR	Bard (C.R.)	J	Ph
BMG	Battle Mountain Gold	J	A & C
BOL	Bausch & Lomb	J	A
BAX	Baxter International	F	C
BSC	Bear Stearns Cos.	J	C
BDX	Becton Dickinson & Co.	M	Ph
BEL	Bell Atlantic	J	C
BLS	Bell South	J	A
BNL	Beneficial Corp.	J	P
BS	Bethlehem Steel	J	C
BEV	Beverly Enterprises	M	P
BDK	Black & Decker	F	C
BMET	BIOMET	J	C
BBEC	Blockbuster Entertainment	M	A & C
BA	Boeing	F	C
BCC	Boise Cascade	F	C

Symbol	Company	Cycle	Exchange
BLR	Bolar Pharmaceutical	J	C
BN	Borden Inc.	J	P
BCP	Borden Chemicals	F	N
BOW	Bowater Inc.	M	P
BMY	Bristol-Myers	M	C
BP	British Petroleum	J	P
BRO	Broad Inc.	M	Ph
BFI	Browning-Ferris	M	A
BRNO	Bruno's Inc.	F	C
BC	Brunswick Corp.	M	C
BNI	Burlington Northern	J	C
BR	Burlington Resources	F	Ph
CAW	Caesars World	F	A
CAL	CalFed	J	P
CPB	Campbell Soup	F	N
CP	Canadian Pacific	J	Ph
CCB	Capital Cities Communications	F	C
CCL	Carnival Cruise Lines	J	C
CHH	Carter Hawley Hale	F	P
CKE	Castle & Cooke	M	P
CAT	Caterpillar Inc.	F	A
CBS	CBS Inc.	F	C
CNT	Centel Corp.	J	A
CX	Centerior Energy	F	P
CTUS	Cetus Corp.	J	A
CHA	Champion International	M	C
CHM	Champion Spark Plug	M	N
CHRS	Charming Shoppes	J	Ph
CMB	Chase Manhattan	M	A
CHL	Chemical Banking Corp.	M	A
CHW	Chemical Waste Management	M	A
CHV	Chevron Corp.	M	A
CHPS	Chips & Technologies	J	A
CCN	Chris-Craft Industries	J	C
C	Chrysler Corp.	J	C
CB	Chubb Corp.	J	N
CI	CIGNA Corp.	J	C
CMZ	Cincinnati Milacron	F	Ph

Symbol	Company	Cycle	Exchange
CPX	Cineplex Odeon	J	Ph
CKP	Circle K Corp.	J	P
CC	Circuit City Stores	J	P
CIR	Circus Circus	M	A
CCI	Citicorp	J	C
CSOU	Citizens & Southern Corp.	F	A
CLX	Clorox Co.	J	Ph
CNA	CNA Financial	F	A
CNW	CNW Corp.	J	C
CGP	Coastal Corp.	M	A & C
KO	Coca-Cola	F	C
CCE	Coca-Cola Enterprises	F	C
CL	Colgate Palmolive	F	C
CG	Columbia Gas	F	A
KPE	Columbia Pictures	J	A
CSP	Combustion Engineering	M	P
CMCSA	Comcast Corp.	J	Ph
CDO	Comdisco Inc.	J	P
CBU	Commodore International	F	Ph
CWE	Commonwealth Edison	F	C
CMY	Community Psychiatric	J	Ph
CPQ	Compaq Computer	J	P
CMP	Comprehensive Care	J	Ph
CA	Computer Associates	J	C
CSC	Computer Sciences	M	C
CQ	ComSat	J	Ph
CAG	ConAgra Inc.	M	A
ED	Consolidated Edison	F	A
CNF	Consolidated Freightways	M	N
CNG	Consolidated Natural Gas	J	A
CPER	Consolidated Papers	J	P
CRR	Consolidated Rail	J	Ph
CTC	Contel Corp.	J	A
CIC	Continental Corp.	F	Ph
CDA	Control Data	F	C
COO	Cooper Companies	J	A
CBE	Cooper Industries	J	A
CTB	Cooper Tire	F	Ph
ACCOB	Coors (Adolph)	J	P

Symbol	Company	Cycle	Exchange
GLW	Corning Glass	F	C
COST	Costco Wholesale	J	A
CPC	CPC International	J	P
CYR	Cray Research	M	P
CRL	Crossland Savings	M	A
CSX	CSX Corp.	F	P
CAVN	CVN Companies	J	A
CYM	Cyprus Minerals	J	C
DAZY	Daisy Systems	J	P
DCN	Dana Corp.	J	N
DGN	Data General	M	P
DPC	Dataproducts Corp.	J	P
DH	Dayton Hudson	J	P
DE	Deere & Co.	M	A
DAL	Delta Air Lines	J	C
DLX	Deluxe Corp.	J	P
DTE	Detroit Edison	J	Ph
DEX	Dexter Corp.	J	A
DRM	Diamond Shamrock	J	C
DBD	Diebold Inc.	F	C
DCA	Digital Communications	F	N
DEC	Digital Equipment	J	A & C
DIS	Disney (Walt)	J	A & C
D	Dominion Resources	J	Ph
DNY	Donnelly & Sons	M	A
DOV	Dover Corp.	M	A
DOW	Dow Chemical	M	C
DJ	Dow Jones	M	Ph
DBRN	Dress Barn	J	C
DI	Dresser Industries	J	Ph
DRY	Dreyfus Corp.	J	C
DUK	Duke Power	J	Ph
DNB	Dun & Bradstreet	F	A
DD	duPont	J	A & C
EFU	Eastern Gas & Fuel	J	Ph
EK	Eastman Kodak	J	C
ETN	Eaton Corp.	J	C
ECH	Echlin Inc.	M	P
ECO	Echo Bay Mines	J	P

Symbol	Company	Cycle	Exchange
AGE	Edwards (A.G.)	F	C
EGG	EG&G Inc.	M	Ph
EMR	Emerson Electric	M	A
EMH	Emhart Corp.	J	N
EC	Engelhard Corp.	J	C
ENE	Enron Corp.	J	C
ENS	ENSERCH Corp.	F	P
ENVR	Envirodyne Industries	M	Ph
XON	Exxon Corp.	J	C
EY	Ethyl Corp.	J	P
ESY	E-Systems	F	P
FNM	Fannie Mae	M	Ph
FDX	Federal Express	J	C
FMO	Federal-Mogul	J	P
FBO	Federal Paper Board Co.	J	P
FFC	Fireman's Fund	M	C
FNB	First Chicago	J	C
FEXC	First Executive	J	Ph
I	First Interstate	J	C
FRM	First Mississippi	J	P
FTU	First Union Corp.	J	P
FLE	Fleetwood Enterprises	F	A
FLR	Fluor Corp.	J	C
FMC	FMC Corp.	F	N
F	Ford Motor	M	C
FRX	Forest Labs	F	C
FWC	Foster Wheeler	J	P
FPL	FPL Group	M	Ph
FTX	Freeport-McMoRan	F	C
FRP	Freeport-McMoRan Res.	M	A
FQA	Fuqua Industries	M	C
GAF	GAF Corp.	J	Ph
GCI	Gannett Co.	J	Ph
GPS	Gap Inc.	M	C
GY	GenCorp	M	C
GCN	General Cinema	F	C
GD	General Dynamics	F	C
GE	General Electric	M	C
GRL	General Instrument	M	Ph

Symbol	Company	Cycle	Exchange
GIS	General Mills	J	P
GM	General Motors	M	C
GME	General Motors EDS	M	Ph
GRN	General Re Corp.	M	A
GSX	General Signal	F	Ph
GNE	Genetech Inc.	J	C & P
GEN	Genrad Inc.	M	Ph
GPC	Genuine Parts	F	P
GCG	Georgia Gulf Corp.	F	Ph
GP	Georgia-Pacific	J	Ph
GEB	Gerber Products	J	A
GRB	Gerber Scientific	M	Ph
GFSA	Giant Foods	M	A
GIBG	Gibson Greetings	M	Ph
GS	Gillette Co.	M	A
GLX	Glaxo Holdings	F	A
GLN	GLENFED Inc.	J	A
GNG	Golden Nugget	F	A
GVF	Golden Valley Microwave	J	A
GDW	Golden West Financial	F	Ph
GR	Goodrich	F	C
GT	Goodyear Tire	J	A
GULD	Goulds Pumps	M	N
GRA	Grace (W.R.)	F	A
GAP	Great Atlantic & Pacific	J	A
GNN	Great Northern	J	C
GWF	Great Western Financial	J	C
G	Greyhound	J	A
GRO	Grow Group	F	P
GQ	Grumman Corp.	J	C
GTE	GTE Corp.	M	A
HRB	H & R Block	J	A
HAL	Halliburton Co.	J	C
HAN	Hanson Industries	M	C
HBJ	Harcourt Brace	J	A
HPH	Harnischfeger	F	Ph
HRS	Harris Corp.	F	C
HAS	Hasbro Corp.	J	P
HBOC	HBO & Co.	J	P

Symbol	Company	Cycle	Exchange
HL	Hecla Mining	M	A
HNZ	Heinz (H.J.)	M	C
HP	Helmerich & Payne	M	N
HPC	Hercules Inc.	M	A
HSY	Hershey Foods	F	A
HWP	Hewlett-Packard	F	C
HLT	Hilton Hotels	J	P
HIT	Hitachi	J	C
HIA	Holiday Corp.	F	C
HFF	Holly Farms	J	C
HD	Home Depot	F	Ph
HFD	Home Fed Corp.	J	C
HSN	Home Shopping Network	J	C
HM	Homestake Mining	J	C
HMC	Honda Motor	J	Ph
HON	Honeywell Inc.	F	C
HCA	Hospital Corp. of America	J	P
HTN	Houghton Mifflin	J	P
HI	Household International	J	A
HOU	Houston Industries	M	N
HUM	Humana Inc.	F	C
ITW	Illinois Tool Works	M	Ph
ICI	Imperial Chemical	J	N
N	Inco Ltd.	J	A
IRIC	Information Resources	F	C
IR	Ingersoll Rand	M	N
IAD	Inland Steel	M	Ph
INTC	Intel Corp.	J	A
INGR	Intergraph Corp.	J	A
IBM	Int. Business Machines	J	C
IFF	International Flavors	F	C
IGL	International Minerals	J	C
IP	International Paper	J	C
IPG	Interpublic Group	J	N
ITEL	Itel Corp.	J	C & P
ITT	ITT Corp.	M	C
JR	James River Corp.	M	N
JERR	Jerrico Inc.	J	P

Symbol	Company	Cycle	Exchange
JLUB	Jiffy Lube	J	P
JNJ	Johnson & Johnson	J	C
KM	K Mart	M	C
K	Kellogg Co.	M	A
KEMC	Kemper Corp.	J	Ph
KMG	Kerr-McGee	J	C
KMB	Kimberly-Clark	J	A
KNDR	Kinder-Care	J	P
KWP	King World Productions	F	P
KRI	Knight-Ridder Inc.	J	Ph
KR	Kroger Co.	J	A
LAC	LAC Minerals	J	C
LLY	Lilly (Eli)	J	A
LTD	Limited Inc.	F	C
LINB	LIN Broadcasting	F	Ph
LIT	Litton Industries	M	C
LIZC	Liz Claiborne	J	C
LK	Lockheed	M	P
LFC	Lomas Financial	M	Ph
LSST	Lone Star Technologies	M	N
LOR	Loral Corp.	J	C
LT	Lorimar-Telepictures	J	C
LOTS	Lotus Development	J	A
LLX	Louisiana Land	F	Ph
LPX	Louisiana-Pacific	F	A
LOW	Lowes Companies	J	Ph
LTR	Lowes Corp.	M	C
LLSI	LSI Logic	J	C
LZ	Lubrizol Corp.	F	Ph
LMED	LyphoMed Inc.	J	A
MAI	M/A-Com	F	A
MNR	Manor Care	J	Ph
MHC	Manufacturers Hanover	J	A
MDA	Mapco Corp.	J	P
MKC	Marion Labs	J	P
MHS	Marriott Corp.	J	Ph
MMC	Marsh & McLennan	J	P
ML	Martin Marietta	M	Ph

Symbol	Company	Cycle	Exchange
MAS	Masco Corp.	J	A
MASX	Masco Industries	J	P
MAT	Mattel Inc.	J	A
MXTR	Maxtor Corp.	J	P
MXS	Maxus Energy	J	P
MA	May Department Stores	M	C
MYG	Maytag Corp.	J	N
MCA	MCA Inc.	F	Ph
MDR	McDermott International	F	Ph
MCD	McDonald's Corp.	M	C
MD	McDonnell Douglas	F	P
MHP	McGraw-Hill	F	Ph
MCIC	MCI Communications	J	C
MCK	McKesson Corp.	F	P
MEA	Mead Corp.	J	C
MCCS	Medco Containment	J	P
MDT	Medtronic Inc.	F	C
MEL	Mellon Bank	M	N
MES	Melville Corp.	F	P
MNTR	Mentor Corp.	J	A & P
MENT	Mentor Graphics	J	A
MRK	Merck & Co.	J	C
MER	Merrill Lynch	J	A & C
MLP	Mesa Ldt. Partnership	J	A
MCRN	Micron Technology	J	A, C & P
MSFT	Microsoft Corp.	J	A & P
MSU	Middle South Util.	M	C
MDW	Midway Airlines	J	C
MLHR	Miller (Herman)	F	N
MINY	MiniScribe Corp.	F	A
MMM	Minnesota M & M	J	C
MINL	Minnetonka Corp.	J	P
MND	Mitchell Energy	M	P
MOB	Mobile Corp.	F	C
MOLX	Molex Inc.	J	C
MTC	Monsanto Co.	J	C
JPM	Morgan (J. P.)	M	Ph
MS	Morgan Stanley Group	F	Ph
MORR	Morrison Inc.	J	N

Symbol	Company	Cycle	Exchange
MTI	Morton Thiokol	J	Ph
MOT	Motorola Inc.	J	A
MUR	Murphy Corp.	F	P
MYL	Mylan Labs	J	A
NLC	Nalco Chemical	M	Ph
NEC	National Education Corp.	J	C
NME	National Medical	F	A
NPD	National Patent	M	P
NSM	National Semiconductor	F	A & C
NCB	NCNB Corp.	F	Ph
NCR	NCR Corp.	M	C
NSCO	Network Systems	J	A
NGC	Newmont Gold	F	Ph
NEM	Newmont Mining	M	Ph
NYT	N.Y. Times	J	P
NMK	Niagara Mohawk	M	A
NIKE	NIKE Inc.	J	P
NBL	Noble Affiliates	F	A
NOBE	Nordstrom Inc.	J	A
NSC	Norfolk Southern	M	C
NT	Northern Telecom	M	C
NOC	Northrop Corp.	F	C
NRT	Norton Co.	J	C
NOVL	Novell Inc.	F	A
NVO	Novo Industries	F	A
NOXLB	Noxell Corp.	F	C
NWA	NWA Inc.	J	C
NYN	NYNEX	J	N
OXY	Occidental Petroleum	F	C
ODR	Ocean Drilling	F	A
OG	Ogden Corp.	F	C
OGIL	Ogilvy Group	F	A
OMT	Ohio Mattress Co.	J	Ph
OLN	Olin Corp.	F	A
OMCM	Omnicom Group	J	P
ORCL	Oracle Systems	M	C
OCF	Owens-Corning	M	Ph
PCAR	Paccar Inc.	F	N
PET	Pacific Enterprises	J	A

Symbol	Company	Cycle	Exchange
PCG	Pacific G & E	M	N
PAC	Pacific Telesis	J	P
PWJ	PaineWebber Group	J	C
PLL	Pall Corp.	M	C
PEL	Panhandle Eastern	J	Ph
PNS	Pansophic Systems	F	C
PCI	Paramount Communications	M	C
PH	Parker-Hannifin	F	Ph
PGU	Pegasus Gold	F	C
PC	Penn Central	M	Ph
JCP	Penney (J. C.)	F	A
PSM	Pennwalt Corp.	J	A
PZL	Pennzoil Co.	J	C
PBY	Pep Boys	J	N
PEP	PepsiCo Inc.	J	C
PKN	Perkin-Elmer	M	P
PST	Petrie Stores	M	Ph
PFE	Pfizer, Inc.	M	A
PD	Phelps Dodge	J	A
PE	Philadelphia Electric	J	P
MO	Philip Morris	M	A
PHL	Philips Industries	F	Ph
PHG	Philips NV	J	N
P	Phillips Petroleum	F	A
PICN	Pic 'N' Save	J	P
PHYB	Pioneer Hi-Bred	M	A
PBI	Pitney Bowes	J	A
PCO	Pittston Co.	F	Ph
PDG	Placer Dome Inc.	M	Ph
PNC	PNC Financial	F	Ph
PRD	Polaroid Corp.	J	C & P
PPG	PPG Industries	F	Ph
PCST	Precision Castparts	F	C
PCLB	Price Co.	J	P
PRM	Prime Computer	M	A
PDQ	Prime Motor Inns	J	P
PA	Primerica	M	Ph
PG	Procter & Gamble	J	A
PEG	Public Service Enterprises	M	A

Symbol	Company	Cycle	Exchange
OAT	Quaker Oats	J	Ph
KSF	Quaker State	M	A
CUE	Quantum Chemical	F	A
QNTM	Quantum Corp.	F	N
RAL	Ralston Purina	M	C
RYC	Raychem Corp.	J	P
RTN	Raytheon Co.	F	C
RBK	Reebok International	J	A & P
RLM	Reynolds Metals	F	P
RAD	Rite Aid	J	Ph
RJR	RJR Nabisco	F	C
ROAD	Roadway Services	J	P
ROK	Rockwell International	J	C
ROH	Rohm & Haas	J	A
RHR	Rohr Industries	M	Ph
REN	Rollins Environmental	J	P
ROR	Rorer Corp.	J	A
RD	Royal Dutch Petroleum	F	A
RPOW	RPM, Inc.	M	C
RBD	Rubbermaid	F	P
R	Ryder Systems	F	P
SFCD	SafeCard	J	P
SAFC	SAFECO Corp.	F	N
SK	Safety-Kleen Corp.	M	Ph
STJM	Saint Jude Medical	J	C
STPL	Saint Paul Companies	J	C
SLM	Sallie Mae	J	C
SB	Salomon, Inc.	J	Ph
SFX	Santa Fe Southern	M	A
SLE	Sara Lee Corp.	J	A
SCE	SCECORP.	J	P
SGP	Schering-Plough	F	P
SLB	Schlumberger Ltd.	F	C
SCIS	SCI Systems	J	C
SFA	Scientific-Atlanta	M	P
SPP	Scott Paper	J	Ph
SGAT	Seagate Technology	M	A
VO	Seagram Co.	F	P
S	Sears, Roebuck	J	C

Symbol	Company	Cycle	Exchange
SPC	Security Pacific	M	Ph
SRV	Service Corp.	F	Ph
SME	Service Merchandise	J	Ph
SHC	Shaklee Corp.	J	A
SMED	Shared Medical Systems	J	P
SNC	Shawmut National Corp.	M	A
SC	Shell Transport	F	C
SHW	Sherwin-Williams	M	C
SHONC	Shoney's Inc.	J	P
SKY	Skyline Corp.	F	C
SKB	SmithKline-Beckman	M	P
SNA	Snap-on Tools	M	A
SNT	Sonat Inc.	J	A
SONO	Sonoco Products	J	P
SNE	Sony Corp.	J	P
SO	Southern Co.	F	C
LUV	Southwest Airlines	M	C
SBC	Southwestern Bell	J	P
SQB	Squibb Corp.	J	C
SWK	Stanley Works	J	P
STO	Stone Container	M	P
STRA	Stratus Computer	J	P
SBRU	Subaru of America	M	Ph
SUN	Sun Co.	F	Ph
SUNW	Sun Microsystems	J	P
SVU	Super Valu Stores	J	Ph
SBL	Symbol Technologies	J	A
SYN	Syntex Corp.	M	C
SYY	Sysco Corp.	F	N
TMB	Tambrands Inc.	J	N
TDM	Tandem Computers	J	A
TAN	Tandy Corp.	J	A & C
TBY	TCBY Enterprises	J	P
TEK	Tektronix Inc.	M	C
TCOMA	Tele-Communications	J	A
TCRD	Telecredit Inc.	M	C
TDY	Teledyne Inc.	J	C & P
TLR	Telerate, Inc.	J	N
TLXM	Telxon Corp.	M	C

Symbol	Company	Cycle	Exchange
TIN	Temple-Inland	F	A
TGT	Tenneco Inc.	F	A
TER	Teradyne Inc.	J	P
TSO	Tesoro Petroleum	F	Ph
TX	Texaco Inc.	J	A
TET	Texas Eastern Corp.	J	Ph
TXN	Texas Instruments	J	C
TXU	Texas Utilities	J	P
TXT	Textron Inc.	M	Ph
COMS	3Com Corp.	J	P
TL	Time Inc.	M	Ph
TMC	Times Mirror	M	N
TMK	Torchmark Corp.	F	A
TOY	Toys 'R' Us	M	C
TA	Transamerica Corp.	F	Ph
E	Transco Energy Co.	F	N
TIC	Travelers Corp.	F	P
TRB	Tribune Co.	F	C
TY	Tri-Continental	M	Ph
TRN	Trinity Industries	J	A
TNV	Trinova Corp.	F	Ph
TRW	TRW Inc.	J	A
TW	TW Services	F	P
TWEN	20th Century Industries	J	P
TYC	Tyco Labs	J	Ph
TYSNA	Tyson Foods	J	P
UAL	UAL Corp.	F	C
UN	Unilever N.V.	F	A
UCC	Union Camp	M	C
UK	Union Carbide	J	A
UNP	Union Pacific	F	Ph
UIS	Unisys Corp.	J	A & C
UTX	United Technologies	F	C
UT	United Telecommunications	F	Ph
UCL	Unocal Corp.	J	P
UPJ	Upjohn Co.	J	C
USR	U.S. Shoe	J	Ph
USW	US West	J	A
U	USAir Group	M	P

Symbol	Company	Cycle	Exchange
FG	USF&G Corp.	J	Ph
USG	USG Corp.	M	C
UST	UST Inc.	F	C
X	USX Corp.	J	A
VLO	Valero Energy	M	A
VAR	Varian Assoc.	F	A
VEE	Veeco Instruments	M	P
VFC	VF Corp.	F	N
VC	Vista Chemical Co.	M	P
WAG	Walgreen Co.	J	A
WMT	Wal-Mart Stores	M	C
WANB	Wang Labs-Class B	J	P
WCI	Warner Communications	F	C
WLA	Warner-Lambert	J	A
WMX	Waste Management	F	Ph
WFC	Wells Fargo	J	A
WEN	Wendy's International	M	P
WPM	West Point-Pepperell	J	C
WDC	Western Digital	J	P
WX	Westinghouse Electric	J	A
W	Westvaco Corp.	J	P
WY	Weyerhaeuser	J	C
WHR	Whirlpool Corp.	M	C
WH	Whitman Co.	M	C
WMTT	Willamette Industries	F	N
WMB	Williams Companies	F	C
WND	Windmere Corp.	J	P
WGO	Winnebago Industries	J	C
Z	Woolworth (F. W.)	F	Ph
WTHG	Worthington Industries	M	Ph
WWY	Wrigley Co.	M	A
WYS	Wyse Technology	J	A
XRX	Xerox Corp.	J	C & P
Yell	Yellow Freight Systems	M	C
ZY	Zayre Corp.	J	C
ZE	Zenith Electronics	F	A

The list of exchange-traded options is subject to frequent change. Contracts covering new securities are added and mergers between existing companies often result in the elimination of contracts. In addition, companies may change their corporate name, resulting in an adjustment in the location of the option prices listing in the newspapers. Up-to-date information can be obtained from the Options Clearing Corporation.

Glossary

Aggregate Exercise Price. The total dollar amount that would change hands if an equity option were exercised. To determine this amount, multiply the number of shares in the contract by the exercise (strike) price.

American Stock Exchange. One of five registered stock exchanges in the United States on which equity options are traded.

At the Money. When the exercise price of an option and the market price of the underlying security are the same, the option is "at the money."

Buyer. The purchaser of options contracts.

Call. An option granting the holder the right to purchase the underlying security under specific terms and conditions.

Cash Dividend. A payment made to a stockholder of a corporation of a fixed amount of money for each share owned.

CBOE. See Chicago Board of Options Exchange

Chicago Board of Options Exchange (CBOE). A registered exchange on which equity options are traded. The CBOE was the first exchange to trade equity options.

Class. All options of the same type (put or call) which cover the same underlying security.

Closing Purchase. The purchase of an equity option that results in the reduction or elimination of a prior short position.

Closing Sale. The sale of an equity option that results in the reduction or elimination of a prior long position.

Combination. A put or call on the same security in which either the strike price and/or the expiration month are different. A combination can be either a long combination or a short combination.

Covered Writer. The short seller of an option who has an offsetting position that will enable him to complete the contract if it is exercised.

Currency Option. An options contract in which the underlying product is a foreign currency.

Delta. An options derivative that measures the anticipated percentage of change in the premium as related to a change in the market price of the underlying security.

Disclosure Statement. A document supplied to clients that details the characteristics and risks of listed options.

Ex-Dividend Date. The date on which the purchaser of a stock will no longer be entitled to a forthcoming dividend. This date is generally the fourth business day prior to the record date established by the corporation paying the dividend.

Exercise Price (Strike Price). The dollar price per share at which the holder of an equity option may sell (put) or purchase (call) the shares of the underlying security.

Expiration Month. The calendar month in which an equity option will cease to be capable of exercise.

Expiration Time. The date and time within the expiration month at which the option expires.

FIFO. See First in, First out.

First in, First out (FIFO). An acceptable method by which a securities dealer may determine which of his clients will be assigned an exercise notice on an option. The first client who wrote the contract will receive the first assignment of exercise.

Gamma. An options derivative that measures the expected change in an options delta factor that will accompany a change in the market value of the underlying security.

Index Options. Puts or calls that are based on an index of stock values. An index measures the overall value of a large group of stocks. Index options are settled in cash rather than by delivery of the actual securities.

Interest Rate Options. Puts and calls in which the underlying product is debt rather than equity securities. Interest rate options are based on bills, notes, and bonds issued by the U.S. Treasury.

In the Money. A term used to describe an option that has an intrinsic value based on the strike price of the option and the market price of the underlying security.

Long. A long term used to describe a position in which a person owns a security or options contract.

Market Maker. A member of the Chicago Board of Options Exchange who deals in specific options contracts on the exchange floor. The market maker acts only as a principal, buying and selling for his own account.

New Account Document. A document that must be prepared prior to the opening of an account to trade in options. The document must include all necessary information regarding the account, including net worth, annual income, and investment objectives.

New York Stock Exchange. One of the five registered stock exchanges in the United States on which equity options are traded.

OCC. See Options Clearing Corporation.

Opening Purchase. A transaction in which a client buys an equity option for the purpose of initiating a long position or increasing a current long position in that option.

Opening Sale. A transaction in which a client sells an equity option for the purpose of initiating a short position or increasing a current short position in that option.

Option. A contract which grants the holder the right to purchase (call) or sell (put) a specific number of shares of a security at a fixed price for a period of time.

Options Agreement. A document that must be signed by all options clients by which they agree to be bound by all regulations covering the trading and settlement of options contracts.

Options Clearing Corporation (OCC). A clearing house established to handle the settlement and clearing of options contracts. The OCC is responsible for these functions for equity options, index options, currency options, and interest rate options.

Order Book Official. An employee of the CBOE who maintains a listing of orders from clients to buy or sell equity options. The order book official acts as agent for these clients.

Out of the Money. A term used to describe an option that has no intrinsic value based on the strike price of the option and the market price of the underlying security.

Pacific Stock Exchange. One of five registered stock exchanges in the United States on which equity options are traded.

Philadelphia Stock Exchange. One of five registered stock exchanges in the United States on which equity options are traded.

Premium. The fee paid by the purchaser of an option to the seller of that contract. The premium represents the number of dollars paid for each unit of the contract.

Put. A contract that gives the holder the privilege to sell the underlying security under specific terms and conditions.

Quotation. The highest price that will currently be paid to purchase an option contract (bid) and the lowest current price at which that contract is offered for sale (offer).

Random Selection. A method used to assign exercise notices of options contracts against writers of the contract.

Record Date. The date on which the owner of a stock must be listed on the records of a corporation in order to be entitled to a dividend to be paid by that corporation.

Seller. The party to a transaction in an option who sells the contract to the purchaser.

Series. All options of the same class having both the same strike price and the same expiration date.

Short Position. A position arising from the sale of an options contract by a party who does not own the contract.

Short Sale. The sale of an options contract which the selling party does not own. The short seller of an options contract is called the "writer."

Specialist. A member of the American Stock Exchange who transacts business in options contracts. The specialist can act as either agent or principal in these transactions.

Spread. An options strategy in which the trader is long one series in a class of options and short a different series in the same class. Spreads are established at either credits or debits.

Stock Dividend. A payment by a corporation to shareholders in the form of additional shares rather than cash.

Stock Split. A change in the capitalization of a corporation in which the number of outstanding shares is increased by a specific amount. The par value of the shares is reduced accordingly.

Straddle. An options strategy which contains both a put and a call on the same security with the same strike price and the same expiration month. A straddle can be either a long straddle or a short straddle.

Strap. An options strategy consisting of one put and two calls on the same security with the same strike price and same expiration month. In a strap the client can be either long or short the options.

Strike Price. See Exercise Price.

Strip. An options strategy consisting of two puts and one call on the same security with the same strike price and same expiration month. The client can be either long or short the strip.

Theta. An options derivative that measures the erosion of an option premium due to the passage of time.

Type. There are two types of options—puts and calls.

Uncovered Writer. The short seller of an options contract who does not have an offsetting position that will allow him to fulfill the contract if it is exercised.

Underlying Security. The common stock of a corporation that is the subject of an equity options contract.

Vega. An options derivative that measures the effect on an options premium caused by a change in the volatility factor of the underlying security.

Writer. The short seller of an options contract. The writer can either be covered or uncovered (naked).

Index